FINDING GOD AGAIN

FINDING GOD AGAIN

SPIRITUALITY FOR ADULTS

John J. Shea

ROWMAN & LITTLEFIELD PUBLISHERS, INC.
Lanham • Boulder • New York • Toronto • Oxford

ROWMAN & LITTLEFIELD PUBLISHERS, INC.

Published in the United States of America
by Rowman & Littlefield Publishers, Inc.
A wholly owned subsidiary of The Rowman & Littlefield Publishing Group, Inc.
4501 Forbes Boulevard, Suite 200, Lanham, Maryland 20706
www.rowmanlittlefield.com

PO Box 317
Oxford
OX2 9RU, UK

British Library Cataloguing in Publication Information Available

Library of Congress Cataloging-in-Publication Data

Shea, John J., 1940-
    Finding God again : spirituality for adults / John J. Shea.
        p. cm.
    Includes bibliographical references and index.
    ISBN 0-7425-4214-9 (hardcover : alk. paper) — ISBN 0-7425-4215-7 (pbk. : alk.
paper)
    1. God. 2. Image of God. 3. Spirituality. I. Title.
    BT103.S44 2004
    248.8'4—dc22

                                                                2004030313

∞™ The paper used in this publication meets the minimum requirements of
American National Standard for Information Sciences—Permanence of Paper
for Printed Library Materials, ANSI/NISO Z39.48-1992.
Manufactured in the United States of America.

ACKNOWLEDGMENTS

I am very grateful to all who helped me with this book, especially:

Neil McGettigan of Villanova University for his invaluable insights on imaging God and for his expert editorial help.

My students at Boston College in the Institute of Religious Education and Pastoral Ministry and the faculty, especially Tom Groome and John McDargh.

My students at Fordham University and especially four of my former colleagues, Janna Heyman, George McCauley, Beverly Musgrave, and Janet Ruffing.

For encouragement, Gary Ahlskog, Tom Beaudoin, Catherine Bernard, Gene Gendlin, W. Norris Clark, Janet Cousins, Rich Gula, Jack Healey, Peter Homans, Anne Kelliher, Brian and Mary Kelty, Joan Kerley, Ann Laszok, Ann Lynch, Paul Morrissey, Dick Nahman, Vin Novak, Paul Philibert, Jim Shea, and Jerry and Ruth Starratt.

All those who helped me find the different people I interviewed for this book.

All those I interviewed. While I have changed some of the particulars in their personal histories for the sake of confidentiality, I have tried to be as faithful as possible to exactly what these interviewees expressed about their imaging of God. To do these interviews—with people from different ethnic backgrounds and countries of origin—was a privilege. Often, I felt as though I were walking on sacred ground.

Fordham University in New York City for two Faculty Fellowships.

The Graduate Theological Union, Berkeley, California, for visiting scholar status in 1995.

Gene Lauer of the Hesburgh Sabbatical Program at the Catholic Theological Union, Chicago, Illinois, for hospitality in 2003.

Finally, since much of what I have learned comes from being in supervision for counseling, I would like to thank the wonderful supervisors it has been my privilege to have had over the years: Kevin Mooney, Pierre Turgeon, Kelton Ro-Trock, Arthur Travis, Virginia Mahan, Junie Mayes, Dick Donnenwirth, Angela Montague, and Nancy Bottger.

INTRODUCTION

*To associate the mystery of invitation, the absolute yes
to man's [sic] future, the radical call to eternally abid-
ing love—God—with the hot and cold arbitrary tyrant
of the superego is a matter of grave distortion.*

—John Glaser

With these words, John Glaser touches on what I believe are two
of the most difficult questions that we face in religion as both
women and men.[1] The first question is, how adequate is our imaging
of God for the reality of who God is? The second question is, how adequate is our imaging of God for the reality of who we are? Implicit in
Glaser's words is a number of other questions as well, especially questions about religious growth. Is our imaging of God meant to undergo
transformation as we grow and develop? How can this transformation
happen? And if it is possible for our imaging of God to be transformed, who or what is actually transformed? Is God transformed?
Are we transformed? In religion, can we even separate the self from
God? In religion, are not the self and God meant to develop together?

In our early development, superego images of God—God as a parent-
like, all-powerful, all-knowing, all-loving deity who is also controlling,
rule-issuing, judgmental, guilt-evoking, and at times terrifying—
are hard to avoid. These are the images of God that so often form our
first religious impressions. These are the images of God we so easily

take in from our parents, from organized religion, and from the culture. And these are the images that so often form our beginning relationship with God. To some extent at least, the God of childhood and adolescence is what Glaser describes as "the hot and cold arbitrary tyrant of the superego." In other words, the God of childhood and adolescence is, for many, a Superego God.

There comes a time, however, when, for many of us, the Superego God actually begins to be experienced as "a matter of grave distortion." This God becomes too narrow, or too rigid, or too unreal, or too inadequate to continue holding our trust. This God can no longer mediate all we know from our own experience or make sense of the complexity of our lives. This God cannot seriously respond to the questions that are part of adult reality. This God is not willing to let us take responsibility for ourselves, nor seemingly interested in any kind of real and personal relationship. Unfortunately, however, when this time comes, instead of graciously allowing itself to be transformed, the Superego God often turns into an impenetrable obstacle that blocks the way of adult religion. Glaser has it right when he says, "Such a God deserves to die."[2]

In this book, I am proposing that there are two dramatically different paradigms of imaging God. There is the paradigm of "The Superego God," which belongs to religion in its early stages of development, and there is the paradigm of "The Living God," which is at the center of adult religion. My interest in writing this book—an interest primarily pastoral and practical—is first in making clear the differences in these two paradigms, and then in offering some suggestions as to how the first paradigm can be transformed into the second. In this book, I am responding to the two basic questions that got me interested initially in wanting to write it. The first question is, *why is our relating to God so often presented as if it were something static and not something meant to develop as we ourselves develop and mature?* The second question follows from the first, *why are so many adults still living with a God of childhood and adolescence, a Superego God?*

As I grappled with these questions, I found that the more I took seriously how we actually develop and how we actually experience God, the more a sense of the underlying structure of these two paradigms of relating to God began to emerge. At the heart of this structure lie the notion and the reality of human *adulthood*. Over time, I have come to understand that an "adult self" is the pivotal reality on which human development depends. I have also come to see that an understanding of an adult self and the way this self is able to image reality is essential for an adequate understanding of our imaging of God. In other words, if we take human development seriously, then we are able to take adulthood seriously. If we take adulthood seriously, then we are able to take religion seriously. As adulthood goes, so goes our imaging of God. This book is about adulthood and religion.

We usually pay little attention to what it means to be adult. We tend to think of adults as those who have finished growing up, as those who have reached eighteen or twenty-one years of age, as those who have settled down and have started a family. In most cultures, adulthood is thought of in chronological terms or as a state in life. Little attention is paid to adult maturity, and likewise, little attention is paid to adult religion. It is as if we just naturally become mature adults and just naturally mature in our religion as well. The truth is, however, that for any number of reasons it may be very difficult for us to become mature adults and to have a mature religion. We have to be nurtured and often we have to struggle heroically to reach adulthood, and the same is true if we are to become adult in our religion.

The first part of what I am proposing is: while we are in the process of growing to adulthood (I call this the "adolescing self"), our ability to image reality is also still growing (I call this "fettered imaging"); an adolescing self with fettered imaging tends to find an adolescing God, a God that is still growing (I call this God the "Superego God"). In diagram, it looks like this:

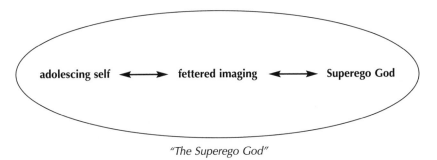

"The Superego God"

These three interacting parts are together in an early form of religion, understanding religion as "that which is about the self and God together." This means that what stage the self is at developmentally and how this self is able to image its reality have a direct bearing on the kind of God the self is able to image. Ultimately, it makes little sense in religion for us to talk about God without taking into account an actual person who is imaging God. However, some of the disciplines that treat religion (especially the disciplines of philosophy and theology) often end up doing just this. They set aside the person who is experiencing God—let alone any developmental understanding of the person—and talk just about God.[3] Other disciplines that talk about religion (especially the disciplines of psychology and anthropology) set aside the God who is experienced and talk just about the person who is supposed to be doing the experiencing.

If we want to consider religion as it is actually experienced, it is important to keep in mind that *religion is about the self and God together*.[4] On the personal level, we only really know God in relation to the self. Augustine had it right back in the fourth century when he prayed, "*noverim me noverim te*" (that I may know myself, that I may know Thee).[5] And it has been said, "The journey into God is the journey into self, and the journey into self is the journey into God." In religion, the self and God go together. This book is a developmental understanding of how they do.

When we are fortunate enough and courageous enough to be able to grow up and become a functioning adult (I call this an "adult self"), our ability to image reality grows up as well and no longer remains fettered (I call this "unfettered imaging"); only on the basis of an adult self with unfettered imaging is it possible, at least in any consistent way, to image a God who is much more than the Superego God (I call this God the "Living God"). In diagram it looks like this:

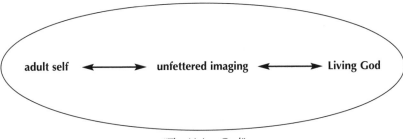

"The Living God"

Unfortunately, many people never realize the transformation from "The Superego God" to "The Living God." For one thing, becoming and then continuing to live as an adult self is no easy thing for some of us, especially if we have had a particularly difficult time growing up or if we live in an affluent, youth-oriented society, a society which invites us to substitute things, achievement, and a separate, self-sufficient autonomy for personal relationships and which views being an adult as akin to dullness, deterioration, and death.

For another thing, the superego imaging of God comes to us so early in life, is so pervasive in the culture, and often is so strongly supported by organized religion that we may be completely unaware that there is anything more than a Superego God. Strangely enough, even if we have had some significant early experiences of a Living God, we may still find the Superego God much too powerful to be transformed. I believe the hegemony the Superego God has over us to be a religious tragedy—the developmental equivalent of the worst idolatries and heresies in the history of Western religion.

Part I of this book describes "The Superego God." First, there is a chapter on "The Adolescing Self," which describes the self on its way to adulthood. This is followed by a chapter on "Imaging and Fettered Imaging," which looks at the person as a developing process of imaging reality. Next, there is a chapter describing "Characteristics of the Superego God." Then there is a chapter on "Adolescing Religion and

Formal Religion," which describes how the adolescing self and the Superego God interact and which describes formal religion. Part I closes with a chapter of "Images of the Superego God," which offers a number of first-hand accounts of the self in relationship with different versions of this God.

Part II of this book describes "The Living God." It begins with a pivotal chapter on "The Adult Self," which carefully describes the structure of this self. This is followed by a chapter on "Unfettered Imaging and Religious Experiencing," which makes the case that an imaging of God that is no longer fettered is really a description of religious experience as an ongoing process. Next, there is a chapter describing "Characteristics of the Living God." Then there is a chapter on "Adult Religion and Integral Spirituality," which describes how the adult self and the Living God are in dialogue and which shows that adult religion is a whole spirituality. Part II closes with a chapter of "Images of the Living God," which offers a number of first-hand accounts of the self in relationship with different versions of this God.

Part III of this book, "Transformation: From 'The Superego God' to 'The Living God,'" looks at how adolescing religion can be transformed into adult religion. This third part of the book has four chapters. First, there is a chapter on "Transformation and Why It Gets So Little Attention." Second, there is a chapter on "What Hinders Transformation." Third, there is a chapter on "What Facilitates Transformation." And finally, there is a chapter of "Images of Transformation" which offers a number of first-hand accounts of the transformation of "the self and God together."

Four last things before we begin:

First, if we find we are living with a Superego God, it is not only important to have an understanding of this God, but it is also important to have some understanding for ourselves as well. It does little good, for example, to berate ourselves for having a Superego God or to pretend we have a different God if this is the one we actually do have. Also, it does little good just to disown this God, unhelpful, troubling, or terrifying as this God may be. The truth is that the Superego God does not usually take rejection very well. What may be helpful is to pay attention to our relationship with God just as it is. When we are with God, just as we experience ourselves to be and just as we find our God is for us, then the relationship may begin to change and to evolve. Things only move from where they are.

Second, in this book I have tried as much as possible to avoid the language of faith, belief, and theology, not to deny the importance of the specific faiths, beliefs, and theologies that you and I may have but to try instead to take seriously the more personal and yet more universal language of religious experience. Unfortunately, the language of faith, belief, and theology often remains general and abstract, pointing to the way God ought to be thought about rather than to the way God actually is experienced.

Third, I have tried to avoid sexist language completely in this book. Some quotes, especially those from a few years ago, use "man," and "he," and "his" instead of nouns, pronouns, and possessive adjectives that are gender inclusive. I use these quotes because of their helpfulness, and I take the points being made to be as applicable for women as they are for men.

Fourth, part of the fun in writing this book is to have been in dialogue—mostly in my own head—with a number of writers from different backgrounds whose work has been insightful, or challenging, or confirming. In an effort to keep what I am trying to say about our imaging of God as readable as possible, I have tried to allow the more scholarly notations to find their way to the endnotes.

NOTES

1. John W. Glaser, "Conscience and Superego: A Key Distinction," in *Conscience: Theological and Psychological Perspectives*, ed. C. Ellis Nelson (New York: Newman, 1973), 177.

2. Glaser, "Conscience and Superego," 177.

3. For a good example of an approach to theology which does *not* neglect the experiencing subject, see Paul J. Philibert, "Readiness for Ritual: Psychological Aspects of Maturity in Christian Celebration," in *Alternative Futures for Worship*, ed. Regis A. Duffy (Collegeville, MN: The Liturgical Press, 1987), 63-121.

4. If I had to give a definition of religion, it would be "that which is about the self and God together." One thing seems clear. If "that which is about the self and God together" is not the starting point of religion, then it is hard to see how it can become its destination down the road.

5. Aurelius Augustinus, *Soliloquies*, II, 1, 1.

I

THE SUPEREGO GOD

THE ADOLESCING SELF

Since the adolescing self is by definition a self on the way to adulthood, it is best to define this self in light of adulthood and to describe it as it actually seems to be on its journey toward that development. Two overall characteristics, which are always found woven together, capture the nature of this self. First, the adolescing self is a *still-forming self*. It is a self still growing, still coming together, still on the way to its own self-possession and coherence. Second, the adolescing self is a *still-dependent self*. As long as the adolescing self is still forming, it remains dependent on significant others and on the mores of the culture for the sense of itself and for knowing how to be and how to relate to others in the wider world in which it lives.

A fuller understanding of the adolescing self as still-forming and still-dependent can be had by a brief, selective look at the thinking of three distinguished developmental psychologists: Carl Rogers, Abraham Maslow, and Erik Erikson. Each of them sees the adolescing self in light of adult development, and each of them has a different perspective to offer on who we really are as we make this developmental journey.

CARL ROGERS AND THE INCONGRUENT SELF

For Carl Rogers, who combines both developmental and therapeutic concerns, the still-forming and still-dependent self—what he would call "the person becoming a self"—is an *incongruent self*. It is a self whose self-concept, that is, "who I consider myself to be," is out of harmony with what the whole organism is actually experiencing. In Rogers' thinking, as a still-forming self, each one of us grows up incongruent because each one of us has developed "conditions of worth," which say things to the self like, "I am lovable when I eat my spinach" or "I am good if I don't get angry." We get these conditions of worth, which are really Rogers' version of the superego, from significant others who love and accept us on condition that we be the way they want us to be.

As long as we are adolescing, therefore, each one of us is a still-dependent self, one still dependent on the approval of others. In fact, Rogers believes the need for love and acceptance from significant others is so strong as we are growing up that we will adopt the meanings and values of others at the expense of what our own organism experiences as meaningful or valuable. Again, this is incongruence. For the sake of approval, the incongruent self denies or distorts parts of its reality in order to be acceptable in the eyes of significant others. The adolescing self is incongruent because its self-concept (what is primarily "the mind") cannot yet include all of what the organism is actually feeling.[1] There is, at least to some extent, a split or a dichotomy between the mind and the body.

To become a whole self is to move from incongruence to congruence. Congruence is having a self that now relates to others as its own source of love and approval, a self that relates to others as its own locus of meaning and value, a self that no longer needs to misperceive its reality, a self that is aware of all that it is feeling, a self in which the mind and the body are now together in harmony. The congruent self, the "fully functioning person" that Rogers speaks of, is an adult self.[2]

ABRAHAM MASLOW AND THE DEFICIENCY SELF

For Abraham Maslow, the still-forming and still-dependent self is a self that is still "becoming." Until a hierarchy of becoming needs can be satisfied, it is, in fact, a *deficiency self*. These needs, which Maslow calls the "basic needs," are first the physiological needs, then the safety and security needs, then love and belonging needs, and finally the need for esteem from others leading to self-esteem. When these basic needs are sufficiently satisfied, then we can speak of a self who is its own "being" and who is no longer dependent on the basic needs for its "becoming."

Maslow is very clear in stating that our perception and our cognition are also in a deficiency mode until the self comes fully into being. In other words, the grasp of reality that the still-forming and still-dependent self is able to have is fettered by the pursuit of whichever of the basic needs is still seeking sufficient satisfaction. If, for example, I am presently negotiating my love and belonging needs, I will tend to see the world in terms of how these needs might be satisfied. My basic physical needs and my need for security, which have already been sufficiently satisfied, will no longer be the focus of my perception, and I will not really be concerned yet with trying to satisfy my esteem needs. For Maslow an adult self is a self with "being" perception and "being" cognition, who is able to relate to others and to the world not out of deficiency but as a full self, now engaged in a process of self-actualization with others in the world.[3]

ERIK ERIKSON AND THE COMING-TO-IDENTITY SELF

Erik Erikson's still-forming and still-dependent self is a *coming-to-identity self*. He sees the development of these characteristics of the adolescing self in five stages. In the first stage, trust versus mistrust, the infant in the first year of life needs to develop a sense of trust by taking into the body all that the mother and others provide through care. In this dependent relating, if it is satisfying enough, the infant begins to trust that the needs of the body can be satisfied and that the world is basically a friendly place. The beginnings of identity and mutuality lie in this initial sense of trust.

In the second stage, autonomy versus shame and doubt, the toddler in the second and third years of life needs to develop a sense of autonomy, a sense that "I am a self." This autonomy is realized through willpower and the ability to be in control of the body in its dependent dealings with others and the emerging world. Others are now experienced as separate from the self. In fact, autonomy sets the initial boundaries of what is self and what is other, and it prefigures the mature sense of identity and mutuality in adulthood.

In the third stage, initiative versus guilt, the young child in the third, fourth, fifth, and sixth years of life now needs to develop a sense of initiative, a sense of what he or she can actually do in the world as an autonomous self. At this stage, both imagination and sexual desire come alive, and the child plays at being an adult. As a way of controlling imagination and sexual desire, the superego, an inner agency of dependence and control, becomes constellated at this time as well. Initiative is the beginning of an imagined adulthood.

In the fourth stage, industry versus inferiority, the school-age child needs to get down to work. This child, in dependent relating with competent adults, must acquire all kinds of knowledge that may be useful in the society, and the child also must develop skills of mastery and relating that will pave the way for adulthood. Industry, which is the ability to work in a purposeful and collaborative way, is the immediate precursor of adult identity and mutuality.

Finally, in the fifth stage, identity versus identity diffusion, the adolescent now needs to bring all the parts of the self into a "reasonably coherent whole" that is able, in Freud's famous phrase, "to love and work." This "reasonably coherent whole," which includes personal, sexual, and social identity, allows for real and fully mutual relating, relating which respects the integrity of the other even as it respects the integrity of the self. For Erikson, it is in the advent of identity in mutuality that the adult self is born.[4]

Although a great deal more would need to be said even to begin to describe adequately the nature of the adolescing self, still with this very brief foray into the thinking of Rogers, Maslow, and Erikson, two points are clear. The first point is that the adolescing self really is a still-forming self and a still-dependent self, one that is yet, as Erikson phrases it, only "the sum of its parts,"[5] a self still needing others for its own becoming. The adolescing self is a self not yet fully formed, not yet integral, not yet able to stand on its own, and not yet able to be fully mutual. The second point is that the ability of the adolescing self to image reality is likewise still-forming and still-dependent. As seen from the perspective of adulthood, the adolescing self's way of perceiving and knowing reality is not as clear, not as full, not as whole, not as contextual, and not as bodily owned as it may later be.

NOTES

1. I use "the mind" in quotations because, although it is a convenient synonym for perceiving, feeling, and knowing on the one hand, on the other, it connotes a special faculty of knowledge that is separate from the body, and as such "the mind" is a very misleading and unhelpful notion. Picking up this connotation, Katherine Nelson, Darah Hensler, and Daniela Plesa, "Entering a Community of Minds," in *Toward a Feminist Developmental Psychology*, ed. Patricia H. Miller and Ellen K. Scholnick (New York: Routledge, 2000), 66, define "the mind" as "a disembodied, autonomous, individually owned information-processing or representational device." In addition, "the mind" has traditionally been thought of as an aspect of the person which is eternal and, for this reason, separate from the body. "The mind is immortal, the body is not," laconically observes Robert D. Romanyshyn, "Alchemy and the Subtle Body of Metaphor," in *Pathways into the Jungian World: Phenomenology and Analytical Psychology*, ed. Roger Brooke (New York: Routledge, 2000), 33.

2. See Carl R. Rogers, "The Therapist's View of the Good Life: The Fully Functioning Person," in *On Becoming a Person* (Boston: Houghton Mifflin, 1961), 184–96.

3. See Abraham H. Maslow, "A Theory of Human Motivation," in *Motivation and Personality*, 2nd ed. (New York: Harper & Row, 1976), 35–58.

4. See Erik H. Erikson, "Eight Ages of Man," in *Childhood and Society*, 2nd rev. and enl. ed. (New York: Norton, 1963), 247–74.

5. Erik H. Erikson, "The Problem of Ego Identity," in *Identity and the Life Cycle* (New York: Norton, 1980), 121.

2

IMAGING AND
FETTERED IMAGING

THE SELF AS A PROCESS OF IMAGING

Central to our understanding of human development at every level
and central to our relating to God is the notion that *the self is a
process of imaging*. Imaging reality is not only just something we do,
but also more importantly, it is at the heart of who we are. Imaging,
which the body does with the help of all its senses, is the way we grasp
and hold on to our reality. It is the linking of the self with all manner
of events and experiences. Imaging is a continuous, developing, bodily process, an ongoing organizing and reorganizing of perceiving and
knowing. In gestalt language, this process of imaging is an ongoing re-
configuration of "the whole," prompted, it seems, by physical matura-
tion, by the complexity of concepts, and by the experience of conflict
and desire. This process of imaging involves becoming more and
more integral, more and more fully human, more and more fully authored by and owned by the developing self.

It is this developing process of imaging that allows each of us to find
coherence in life's experiences. It is as a process of imaging that each
one of us strives to realize meaning—to find it, construct it, challenge
it, affirm it. This process of imaging refuses to be held bound by the
past or the present. It searches out possibilities, it envisions how the
future might be, and it is intimately connected, as Erikson's work suggests, with the foundational virtue of hope.[1] This process of imaging,

as we will see, is at the heart of any spiritual quest, and it is also at the heart of any religious quest.

Curiously enough, the primacy of the bodily process of imaging and its vital connection to the development and functioning of the self seem to receive little direct attention.[2] Typically, this process is portrayed as "the imagination," a somewhat special and subjective faculty, which some of us enthusiastically celebrate and which others quickly disparage in embarrassment. We have, says Amos Wilder, "romantic ideas" of the imagination, seeing it as "something separably aesthetic and irresponsible."[3] For Wilder, however, nothing could be further from the truth. "It is at the level of imagination," he insists, "that any full engagement with life takes place."[4] Rather than enable us to escape from reality, the process of imaging is what connects us to it. *Imaging is how we entertain the real.* Anything but subjective or fanciful, the process of imaging is our way of intelligently engaging and grasping the world. "Unlike fantasy," says Michael Himes, "imagination is not about escaping reality; it is precisely about making things real."[5] In process terms, it is our "way of transforming and renewing the real."[6]

Mark Johnson begins *The Body in the Mind* by saying, "Without imagination, nothing in the world could be meaningful. Without imagination, we could never make sense of our experience. Without imagination, we could never reason toward knowledge of reality."[7] If this is true of experiencing in general, it is also true of our experiencing of God. Sharon Parks makes this point when she says that "the task of the imagination, and particularly of the religious imagination, is *to compose the real.*"[8] Religious reality, whatever that reality may turn out to be for the individual person, is grasped through a process of imaging. In other words, the central meeting place of "the self and God together" is our developing process of imaging.

FETTERED IMAGING

To say that the adolescing self relates to reality in terms of fettered imaging is a hard point to make. All of us either are now, or at some time were, adolescing selves. As adolescing selves we image our reality just as it is to us, and it may not seem fettered at all. This is just the point. It only makes sense to talk about fettered imaging from the perspective of adulthood. But from that perspective, that is, from the perspective of an adult process of imaging, all that goes before that adult process of imaging is incomplete, limited, or less than whole in some way. This is the point Carl Rogers makes when he describes the "incongruent" self as denying or distorting reality. Rogers is speaking from the perspective of the "congruence" of an adult self, and from this standpoint, the process of imaging leading up to congruence is incomplete in some way. This is the point Abraham Maslow makes when he describes the "becoming" self as having a deficiency perception and cognition of reality. Maslow is speaking from the perspective of the "being" of an adult self, and from this viewpoint, the process of imaging leading up to this "being" suffers from developmental deficiencies of one kind or another.

To put this issue more directly, an adolescing self, that is a self that is still-forming and still-dependent, has a still-forming and a still-dependent process of imaging. While we are growing up, our way of imaging reality is necessarily immature. In the formative years of life, when we are still evolving in our ability to perceive and know, we grasp our reality and have our meanings through a process of fettered imaging. Fettered imaging, then, is simply adolescing imaging, the imaging that comes directly from the still-forming and still-dependent adolescing self. Many things go into the makeup of this imaging: cultural understandings, societal norms, parental values, the influence of peers, and formal religious beliefs. All the elements that go into the makeup of the superego are at play. In other words, *an imaging of reality— either borrowed from others or imposed by them—combines with the incompleteness of the adolescing self's own perceptive and cognitive powers to hinder and constrain what may later be a freer, fuller, more complete, and more appropriate imaging of reality.*

THE THREE STRANDS OF FETTERED IMAGING

There are three major, interwoven strands at the core of fettered imaging. They are fantasy, relating in transference, and the logic of objective knowing. All three of these strands are the natural way of imaging of the still-forming and still-dependent adolescing self, and all three of these strands of adolescing imaging can be seen clearly only from the perspective of an adult self. Of the three, the logic of objective knowing is especially influential in the makeup of fettered imaging because it is so strongly supported by an enlightenment culture and by all the contributions of modern science. Interestingly enough, Sigmund Freud weaves all three strands together in his understanding of the imaging of God.

FANTASY

Fantasy, as understood here, is an adolescing process of imaging that makes reality into whatever the adolescing self decides it should be. Often fantasy is in the service of protecting the still-forming and still-dependent self as it faces the wonders and fears of an unfolding world. At first, fantasy may be in the form of bodily desires and magical thinking. For instance, "I can fly like an airplane if I want to" is a good example of early fantasy. Later, fantasy may be in the form of egocentric thinking. A child may feel, for example, "My mother and my father are getting divorced because of me. It's my fault. If I were not so bad this would not be happening." Still later, there may be a bit of fantasy at play when a teenage girl or boy looks in the mirror and says, "I'm the best (or worst) person in the whole school; no one is as incredibly good looking (or ugly) as I am."

Fantasy, as Ronald Grimes observes, is a way of imaging reality that is "self-preoccupied and projective," and this projective part is understood by Grimes as "compensatory," that is, as "growing out of what we lack, what we are unable to own, or own up to."[9] Fantasy "fills in" what is missing so that experience can make emotional and cognitive sense. It tends to substitute, says Paul Pruyser, "tolerable fictions for intolerable reality."[10] It makes the world a more predictable place, often providing what Edward Casey calls "scenes of satisfaction."[11] Fantasy, therefore, is still-forming and still-dependent perception and cognition coming from the wishes, fears, and innocence of the adolescing self. While fantasy presupposes reality of some kind as a backdrop, either it mixes what is real with what is not real, or it fails to distinguish between the two.[12]

While Freud understands religion as a process of imaging, for him it is always a process of fettered imaging. "Religion," says Freud, "is an attempt to master the sensory world in which we are situated by means of the wishful world, which we have developed within us as a result of biological and psychological necessities."[13] As Freud sees it, we image God as a father who keeps us from harm, who provides a moral code for us to live by, and who promises us life after death.[14] For Freud, religion is not a "free use of the imagination, but an anxious search for substitutes to an unpleasant reality."[15] As "an imaginary enlargement of the father figure,"[16] God is simply elaborated in illusion and fantasy. Religion is, in fact, *only* fantasy; it is, in Pruyser's phrase, the "falsification of reality."[17]

However, for an adolescing self still on the way to its own coherence and integrity, some measure of fantasy is quite appropriate. "Illusions are," says Vivienne Joyce, "a necessary part of psychic growth."[18] In order to understand life, the adolescing self is, in fact, necessarily embedded in fantasy, taking from this fantasy what is needed for sustenance, stability, and encouragement. Human development is readily seen as emergence from this kind of embeddedness.[19] As the adolescing self matures, however, and the boundaries of the self continue to form and come into greater possession, fantasy in religion and in other areas of life must gradually be transformed by experience. As this fantasy is worked through and left behind, the Superego God also is able to be worked through and left behind. All of the characteristics of the Superego God, which we will consider in chapter 3, are elaborated in fantasy.

RELATING IN TRANSFERENCE

Relating in transference, which is an adolescing phenomenon akin to fantasy, is understood here as a still-forming and still-dependent mode of relating to others. By relating in transference, to some degree at least, the adolescing self experiences the other person as an object for satisfying his or her own forming and dependency needs. Surfacing as it does in early childhood, relating in transference must gradually be resolved as the adolescing self continues to move toward adult relationships with others. Growing up relationally is a process of "overcoming transference."[20]

As long as relating in transference exists, it remains an incompleteness in our way of knowing and loving others. Mario Jacobi observes:

> It is a fact that in a relationship which we term transference, the Thou as another whole subject hardly does exist as such. The other person is an object for my own needs, desires, fantasies and fears. The other does not have reality as a whole subject but is somehow the carrier of the projection of my own psychic reality. The other person is experienced as a part of myself and is not a Thou in his or her own right.[21]

With transference in the relationship, Jacobi goes on to say, "the pressures of the internal needs create distortions which do violence to the existence and to the wholeness of the other person."[22] There is, he says, "a larger or smaller element of unreality in our conception of the other person's full subjectivity."[23]

If we can substitute "God" for the "other person" Jacobi is referring to, then we can change his quotation to say:

> It is a fact that in a relationship which we term transference, the Thou as another whole subject hardly does exist as such. God is an object for my own needs, desires, fantasies and fears. God does not have reality as a whole subject but is somehow the carrier of the projection of my own psychic reality. God is experienced as a part of myself and is not a Thou in God's own right.

In other words, as Karin Stephen points out, "God is only one of the many forms of transference and all transferences rest on illusion."[24] When we relate to God in transference, we know and depend on a God created, at least to some extent, out of our own concerns and maintained for our own ends. God becomes something of a chameleon, taking on whatever role is called for by the projected needs of the still-forming and still-dependent self.[25] As Peter Homans puts it:

In the formation of the image of God and in the subsequent ways of relating to this image, men [*sic*] collectively project and then attempt to resolve their individual psychic conflicts. All the wishes, longings, and nostalgias—everything unfulfilled, unlived and unexpressed—appear in the guise of the God image.[26]

For Freud, of course, "religion was finally and always a transference phenomenon" because he saw us as trying to relate to a God whom we created out of our own forming and dependency needs.[27] However, for the adolescing self, for the self that is still developing in its knowing and loving of others, relating in transference is a "transitional relationship" that is both necessary and inescapable.[28] It is a way the adolescing self relates to others—especially to others who hold some kind of authority—which is entirely appropriate. In religion and in the other areas of life as well, we must engage, struggle with, and eventually leave behind that which is of transference in our way of relating.[29] In other words, relating in transference must be resolved gradually by ongoing experience so that the adolescing self can become adult. All the characteristics of the Superego God, which we will consider in chapter 3, are the result of relating to God in transference.

THE LOGIC OF OBJECTIVE KNOWING

The logic of objective knowing, although much more than an adolescing phenomenon, has its "time of special ascendancy" as the adolescing self comes to understand the importance of unbiased observation, objectivity, and all the various methodologies of a scientific approach to reality. One of the clearest descriptions of how this logic develops in the adolescing self is in the work of Jean Piaget.[30]

A self-described "genetic epistemologist," Piaget views the development of logical thinking in children and adolescents in the context of solving problems in the "object" world of mathematics and the physical sciences. Thinking is understood in terms of what he calls "operations." Although these operations become increasingly logical, abstract, and formal as our ability to think continues to develop, they are always in terms of the object world; that is, they are always in terms of our relationship to external reality.[31] Reflecting this point, Jonathan Krieger observes, "According to Piaget, a mature concept of the object requires the perception that the object exist in its own right and that it continues to exist separate and independent of the activity of the perceiving subject."[32]

As a way of imaging meant to correct the distortions inherent in fantasy and relating in transference—and as almost their exact opposite—the logic of objective knowing is gradually introduced to the adolescing self. This logic works by focusing exclusively on external reality. In fact, in order to protect the objective knowing of external reality, this logic pays no attention at all to the perceiving subject, a subject that is seen to be the source of distortion, emotional bias, wishful thinking, and superstition. In other words, and somewhat ironically, for reality to be objectively known by a perceiving subject, the perceiving subject is made to disappear.[33] If knowledge is to be objective, it cannot be subjective.

This logic of objective knowing becomes the paradigm of what perception and cognition really are. There are different versions of this logic, but for our purposes it can be summarized in terms of two very basic principles:

1. *What is real is empirical.* What can be known lies in a concretely observable world of sight and sound and sense impression. What can be known can be demonstrated and verified. Knowledge of reality lies in facts that are empirical.
2. *What is real is objective.* What can be known is "out there in the real world," is separate from the knower (this is known as "the subject-object dichotomy"), and is the same for all to observe. What can be known is not influenced by the knower. Knowledge of reality lies in facts that are objective.

A person who applies the logic of objective knowing to God and who judges that God can be empirically and objectively found by this logic might say, for example, "God is not just a figment of my imagination. God is not just some comforting subjective feeling. God is real. God exists. God is out there, an objective part of the real world." The meaning of the logic of objective knowing for religion is unmistakable. God can be known in a way that can be demonstrated and verified, and God can be known in a way that is not influenced by the knower.

Although a sense of God as objectlike has been part of human thinking for millennia, Nicholas Lash points out that in the seventeenth and eighteenth centuries, "the question of God became an empirical affair."[34] At that time, as Lash tells it, "the hunt was on to prove that somewhere, beyond the particular constituents and movements of the world, a thing, a being, might be found to serve as a firm foundation for its existence and explanation of its design."[35] God, of course, became that "thing," that "being," that "firm foundation" of the world. God became, in Lash's words, "the name of an object which can not only be defined but located and coordinated with other facts and objects in the world, and known as they are known."[36] In a logic of object knowing, our measure of the reality of God is both empirical and objective.

In his own unique way, Freud applies the logic of objective knowing to religion. And his judgment is that God *cannot* be empirically and objectively found by this logic. In *The Future of an Illusion*, he proposes, "Religious ideas are teachings and assertions about facts and conditions of external (or internal) reality which tell one something one has not discovered for oneself and which lay claim to one's belief."[37] We might wish to believe that these religious facts are empirical and objective because of the moral order they stand for and because of the consolations they can bring, but, says Freud, we "cannot remain children for ever."[38] He holds that our childish and neurotic reliance on religion must undergo "education to reality."[39] We have to see, he says, that science is "the only road which can lead us to a knowledge of reality outside ourselves."[40]

Because the logic of objective knowing is the hallmark of our modern understanding of the world and because this logic helps to free us from fantasy and illusion, a large part of most systems of education is geared toward helping an adolescing self find empirical, objective, factual, and scientific ways of understanding reality. As we continue to develop, however, and as we find ourselves relating to reality in ways that are more personally meaningful, other ways of knowing that are more actively involving, more empathic, and more interpersonally challenging become increasingly important to us.[41] In other words, the logic of objective knowing, much like fantasy and relating in transference, must be gradually tempered by our experience. As a way for knowing God, this logic must be engaged, struggled with, and eventually left behind.[42] All the characteristics of the Superego God that we are about to consider in the next chapter have their roots, one way or another, in the logic of objective knowing.

NOTES

1. Erik H. Erikson, "The Life Cycle: Epigenesis of Identity," in *Identity: Youth and Crisis* (New York: Norton, 1968), 106.
2. For a helpful exception, see John Dominic Crossan, "Stages in Imagination," in *The Archaeology of the Imagination*, ed. Charles E. Winquist, Thematic Series, *Journal of the American Academy of Religion* 48, no. 2 (1981): 49–62.
3. Amos Niven Wilder, *Theopoetic: Theology and the Religious Imagination* (Philadelphia: Fortress, 1976), 44.
4. Wilder, *Theopoetic*, 2.
5. Michael J. Himes, *Doing the Truth in Love: Conversations about God, Relationships and Service* (New York: Paulist Press, 1995), 137.
6. Ronald L. Grimes, *Deeply into the Bone: Re-inventing Rites of Passage* (Berkeley: University of California Press, 2002), 4.
7. Mark Johnson, *The Body in the Mind: The Bodily Basis of Meaning, Imagination, and Reason* (Chicago: University of Chicago Press, 1987), ix.
8. Sharon Daloz Parks, *Big Questions, Worthy Dreams* (San Francisco: Jossey-Bass, 2000), 106.
9. Grimes, *Deeply into the Bone*, 111.
10. Paul W. Pruyser, "Lessons from Art Theory for the Psychology of Religion," *Journal for the Scientific Study of Religion* 15, no. 1 (March 1976): 6.
11. Edward S. Casey, *Spirit and Soul: Essays in Philosophical Psychology* (Dallas, TX: Spring, 1991), 92.
12. See D. W. Winnicott, *Playing and Reality* (London: Routledge, 1982), 26–37.

13. Sigmund Freud, *New Introductory Lectures on Psychoanalysis*, ed. and trans. James Strachey (New York: Norton, 1965), 168.

14. See Sigmund Freud, *The Future of an Illusion* (Garden City, NY: Anchor, 1964).

15. Paul W. Pruyser, "Sigmund Freud and His Legacy: Psychoanalytic Psychology of Religion," in *Beyond the Classics? Essays in the Scientific Study of Religion*, ed. Charles Y. Glock and Phillip E. Hammond (New York: Harper & Row, 1973), 259.

16. Antoine Vergote, "Confrontation with Neutrality in Theory and Practice," in *Psychoanalysis and Religion*, ed. Joseph H. Smith and Susan A. Handelman (Baltimore: Johns Hopkins University Press, 1990), 82.

17. Paul W. Pruyser, *Between Belief and Unbelief* (New York: Harper & Row, 1974), 190.

18. Vivienne Joyce, "The Play of Illusion as an Opening to the Future of the Self: Reflections of a Religious Clinician Occasioned by Rereading *The Future of an Illusion*," in *Psychotherapy and the Religiously Committed Patient*, ed. E. Mark Stern (New York: Haworth, 1985), 73.

19. It seems that most writers on development, including Sigmund Freud, Jean Piaget, Lawrence Kohlberg, Robert Selman, D. W. Winnicott, and Carl Rogers, have at least an implicit theory of embeddedness. For a more explicit understanding of this notion, see Ernest G. Schachtel, *Metamorphosis: On the Development of Affect, Perception, Attention, and Memory* (New York: Basic Books, 1959); see especially Robert Kegan, *The Evolving Self: Problem and Process in Human Development* (Cambridge, MA: Harvard University Press, 1982).

20. See Karin Stephen, "Relations between the Superego and the Ego," *Psychoanalysis and History* 21, no. 1 (2000): 11–28, for a clear discussion of "overcoming transference" in the service of health and adulthood.

21. Mario Jacobi, *The Analytic Encounter: Transference and Human Relationship* (Toronto: Inner City Books, 1984), 64.

22. Jacobi, *The Analytic Encounter*, 64.

23. Jacobi, *The Analytic Encounter*, 67.

24. Stephen, "Relations between the Superego and the Ego," 19.

25. For various roles of the superego, see Ernst A. Ticho, "The Development of Superego Autonomy," *The Psychoanalytic Review* 59, no. 2 (Summer 1972): 217–33.

26. Peter Homans, "Toward a Psychology of Religion: By Way of Freud and Tillich," in *The Dialogue between Theology and Psychology*, ed. Peter Homans (Chicago: University of Chicago Press, 1968), 65.

27. Peter Homans, "Transference and Transcendence: Freud and Tillich on the Nature of Personal Relatedness," *Journal of Religion* 46, no. 1, pt. 2 (1966): 153.

28. W. W. Meissner, *Psychoanalysis and Religious Experience* (New Haven, CT: Yale University Press, 1984), 172.

29. Murray Stein, *Transformation: Emergence of the Self* (College Station: Texas A&M University, 1998), 70, states, "After forming a relationship and living in it for a time, one expects less projection, less idealization, and resolution of transference or its flight to another person."

30. James W. Fowler, *Stages of Faith: The Psychology of Human Development and the Quest for Meaning* (San Francisco: Harper & Row, 1981), 102, calls Piaget's understanding of cognition a "logic of rational certainty," and he contrasts this logic with a "logic of conviction" in which "the constitution of the knowing self is part of what is at stake."

31. See, for example, Jean Piaget, *Genetic Epistemology* (New York: Norton, 1971).

32. Jonathan Krieger, "The Concept of the Object Scale and Cognitive Style: Measures of Differentiation and Their Relationship to Empathy" (PhD diss., Fordham University, 1988), 20.

33. As William Desmond, *Perplexity and Ultimacy: Metaphysical Thoughts from the Middle* (New York: State University of New York Press, 1995), 67, puts it, "There is an oblivion of the self in the very success of self as objective mind."

34. Nicholas Lash, "Incarnate and Determinate Freedom," in *On Freedom*, ed. Leroy S. Rouner (Notre Dame, IN: University of Notre Dame Press, 1989), 23.

35. Lash, "Incarnate and Determinate Freedom," 23.

36. Lash, "Incarnate and Determinate Freedom," 23.

37. Freud, *Future of an Illusion*, 37.

38. Freud, *Future of an Illusion*, 81.

39. Freud, *Future of an Illusion*, 81. For a helpful understanding of Freud's thinking on objectivity as it relates to the process of imaging, see Paul W. Pruyser, "The Tutored Imagination in Religion," in *Changing Views of the Human Condition*, ed. Paul W. Pruyser (Macon, GA: Mercer University Press, 1987), 101–15.

40. Freud, *Future of an Illusion*, 50.

41. Fraser Watts and Mark Williams, *The Psychology of Religious Knowing* (London: Geoffrey Chapman, 1994), 151, point out, "There are many kinds of knowing, with family resemblances, but each with distinct features.

The relative neglect of this consideration has limited the ability of cognitive psychology to give an account of religious knowing, as indeed of aesthetic cognition, personal insight and much more. These neglected forms of knowing arise in a space that transcends a crude dichotomy into what is objective and what is subjective." See also Jerry H. Gill, *Merleau-Ponty and Metaphor* (Atlantic Highlands, NJ: Humanities Press, 1991), 129: "Reality is thus a symbiosis between the knower and the known, as mediated through action and speech, especially through the metaphoric mode." See also Michael Basseches, *Dialectical Thinking and Adult Development* (Norwood, NJ: Ablex, 1984), 63: "Formal operations cannot be equated with cognitive maturity, because formal operations by themselves are adequate only for dealing with a set of closed-system problems which constitute a very narrow sector of the broad range of problems with which adults are confronted."

42. Again, see Pruyser, "Tutored Imagination in Religion," for one way of understanding how reality is more than what is proposed in what is commonly understood as the "realistic world."

CHARACTERISTICS OF THE SUPEREGO GOD

The God that is related to by an adolescing self with its fettered imaging is a Superego God. This God is—and really could only be—a God not yet fully formed, a God still incomplete, a God not yet whole. From one perspective, this God can take any number of configurations as it comes to be imaged by each of us. This should not be surprising. The Superego God is a product of each adolescing self, each with his or her particular fantasy needs, each with his or her particular transference patterns of relating, and each with his or her particular version of the logic of objective knowing. The Superego God comes to us in any number of shapes and guises. One size does not fit all. At the same time, however, this God has some rather definite characteristics that can be fairly accurately described, and this, I believe, is somewhat surprising. Five such characteristics are offered here, each one reflecting some aspect of how, with fettered imaging, an adolescing self finds a Superego God:

1. The Superego God is a Supreme Being.
2. The Superego God is a God of Law.
3. The Superego God is a God of Belief.
4. The Superego God is a God of Dependency and Control.
5. The Superego God is a God of the Group.

In each of these five characteristics, there is a common dynamic at play between the adolescing self and the Superego God. To begin with, each characteristic is a definite statement that captures the *perception* of what this God actually *is* for someone at the superego level. Along with this definite statement about what this God is, often there is, for the adolescing self, a *promise of security*, which is very comforting. This promise of security is had, however, *on condition* that the adolescing self conforms to what the Superego God expects.

As the relationship between the adolescing self and the Superego God continues to develop, often this God is seen to have a *contradiction* at its very core. It is variously caring and not caring, affirming and not affirming, protecting and not protecting, helpful and not helpful. This contradiction—which in time and especially with further education is often hard to avoid—tends to elicit *ambivalent feelings* and a certain amount of *conflict* in the mind of the adolescing self. Consequently, as long as fantasy, relating in transference, and the logic of objective knowing are still being negotiated, there is usually some kind of modus vivendi adopted by the adolescing self in relating to the Superego God.

Finally, with each of these characteristics of the Superego God, two points need to be kept in mind. First, these characteristics are not completely static. There is limited development within each of one of them from the time of their birth in us around the age of three or four until the advent of adult religious development. Second, these characteristics are not, as some persons seem to think, inherently negative. These characteristics of the Superego God are inherently developmental. They become negative or dysfunctional for us to the degree that they actually impede our adult religious development.

1. The Superego God is a Supreme Being. Perhaps the most basic of all the related characteristics of the Superego God is the perception that this God exists as a very elevated personal object, a God of Superlatives, a Supreme Being. This God, as Thomas Merton describes it, is "a God who is simply 'a being' among other beings, part of a series of beings, an 'object' which can be discovered and demonstrated."[1] However distant from us at the other end of the continuum of existence, this Supreme Being is within what many thinkers call the "subject-object dichotomy." This God is "a being beside others and as such a part of the whole of reality."[2] Although an immensely powerful object that is "over against" us, the Supreme Being is part of an ordered system that is ultimately logical, objective, and contained.

Although "up there" and spatially "outside" the world, this Supreme Being still has complete power over the world. Although thought to be eternal, this God is intensely involved in the workings of time. And although thought to exist as an object, this God cannot be located or seen. The Supreme Being is really a contradiction within itself. It is an immensely powerful object, but not really an object. It is an immensely powerful person, but not really a person. It is both, but it is also neither. And although it is an unchangeable reality, which is utterly different from who we are, at the same time this powerful Supreme Being is often quite human and parental—able to protect, to legislate, and to approve or disapprove as needed.

In its beginnings, the Supreme Being often appears to be a very exalted person, who may at times be loving, or uncaring, or quite interested in conformity, control, and punishment. Later, this Supreme Being usually evolves into something less obviously parental, something more like an abstract source of immense power related to causality and the laws of nature. Throughout the whole time of its tenure, however, this Supreme Being promises security from harm and evil—on condition that we can stand in proper relation to it and respect its authority. This promise of security of the Supreme Being is, as Freud attests, often enormously reassuring.[3] Over time, however, we may develop some ambivalent feelings about this Supreme Being, this God that is so incredibly powerful and that is laced with so many contradictions. In trying to find a way of accommodation with this God, we may experience a great deal of confusion and conflict. In dealing with this God, the adolescing self may adopt a modus vivendi that goes back and forth on a continuum of trust, anxiety, fear, lack of engagement, and complete rejection.

2. *The Superego God is a God of Law.* In what is possibly its most prominent characteristic, this God is perceived to be an absolute authority commanding what must and must not be done. Commenting on the moral power of this God, Gordon Kaufman says, "if God has

spoken, how can we lowly humans raise any questions, or why should we want to?"[4] If the Superego God is divine law, then the adolescing self relates to this God through obedience to the law. It is as if, as Nicholas Harvey puts it, "morality has become God."[5] Morality and religion go together. The God of Law is a God of Obedience because the essence of morality consists of carrying out all the commands the God of Law imposes. At the superego level, in fact, religion is always in the context of morality, and this morality is, in Lawrence Kohlberg's framework, always either conventional or preconventional, having to do primarily with either conformity to societal rules or with avoiding punishment.[6]

While usually patient and acting with considerable restraint, the God of Law is often found to be a God of Guilt, evoking terrifying fear and capable of unleashing tremendous judgment and powerful condemnation if we should disobey. Over time, however, this God of Law is often seen to be a contradiction. On the one hand, this God is presented as kindly and benevolent, but on the other hand, this God is an all-seeing judge from whose scrutiny it is impossible for us to hide our shame and guilt. On the one hand, this God is supposed to be quite loving, but on the other hand, this God can be quite coercive, willing to employ whatever external or internal force may be required for us to mend our ways. Moreover, this God of Law is also supposed to reward the good and to punish the wicked. Often, however, it seems to work out just the opposite. In fact, the God of Law often appears to be two Gods, a God of Good and a God of Evil. This divided deity stands over against the adolescing self, mirroring this self's own dividedness and moral failure. And because the God of Law holds us in "credit-debit bondage,"[7] this God is always a God of Conditional Acceptance.

In its beginnings, the God of Law is often what John Glaser describes as a "hot and cold arbitrary tyrant"; that is, this God rewards what it sees as good and punishes what it sees as bad.[8] Later on, this God is seen as issuing a whole set of laws and rules and obligations, which become the substance of conventional morality. Throughout the whole time of its authority, however, the God of Law holds out the promise of security. This God will protect us from harm, will hold us in good standing, and will even relieve us of our guilt—on condition, of course, that we can faithfully carry out all that it commands, or, when moral failure does occur, that we can make appropriate amends. The promise of security of the God of Law is often enormously reassuring to us. Over time, however, the adolescing self may develop ambivalent feelings about this God of Law, which stands so often as God of Perfection, as an "implacable judge who has impossible and rigid standards."[9] We may experience a great deal of conflict in trying to find a way of accommodation with this God whose commands are such a constant reminder of our personal weakness and inadequacy. In dealing with this God, the adolescing self often adopts a modus vivendi that, in addition to the use of a variety of guilt-relieving strategies, goes back and forth between proper compliance and isolating disobedience.

3. *The Superego God is a God of Belief.* This God is thought to exist in any number of beliefs, beliefs that have two essential components. First, there are facts we know about the Supreme Being, and these facts are objective. Second, the facts we know about the Supreme Being are held with at least some amount of emotional loyalty to the authority that supports and conveys them. "Religious ideas are," as Freud puts it, "teachings and assertions about facts,"[10] and the "believer is bound to the teachings of religion by certain ties of affection."[11] Often this God of Belief turns into a God of Orthodoxy. The right beliefs easily become the essence of religion, and, therefore, the adolescing self possesses the Superego God by holding the right beliefs. Often this God of Belief is also a God of the Mind, because this God is grasped by rational thinking and can be defined with the carefully nuanced logic of objective knowing. We "become convinced," says Mark Taylor, "that the essence of religious faith can be objectively defined in formal doctrines and discursive teaching presented by priests and professors. From this perspective, the task of the believer involves, at most, the mastery of objective doctrine and teaching."[12]

Although it seems very important to grasp the God of Belief in just the right propositions, we often find a great deal of contradiction in this God of Belief. This God, which is the object of fact, is also, as we have seen, the object of fantasy. Over time, propositions which those in authority say must be accepted may have little if anything to do with satisfying the needs of our fettered imaging. Moreover, some of the propositions about this God of Belief may convey ideas that seem to be directly opposed to the ideas of other propositions. Some propositions, which are said to be objective and easily verifiable, do not seem to get satisfactorily verified at all. The religious authorities often cannot agree among themselves as to what would count as proper evidence. While statements about God purport to have a common meaning for all, their meanings often vary significantly from individual to individual and from group to group.

In the beginning, the God of Belief seems very parental. "Beliefs," as Pruyser says, "are derived love and hate objects, behind which stand real human love and hate objects of flesh and blood."[13] Later, this God of Belief often becomes more abstract, more logically coherent, and more propositional—although not necessarily less emotionally powerful. Throughout the whole time of its authority, however, this God of Belief promises us protection from a terrible wasteland of confusion, idolatry, and abandonment—on condition, of course, that the adolescing self is unquestioning in holding the proper beliefs. This promise of protection is often enormously reassuring to us. We may have ambivalent feelings, however, about this God of Belief who must be understood in just the right way and whose actions must not be doubted, and we may experience a great deal of conflict in finding out which group has the truth and which facts must be believed. In dealing with this God, the adolescing self often adopts a modus vivendi that goes back and forth on a continuum of trust, confusion, doubt, and disbelief.

4. The Superego God is a God of Dependency and Control. It is the God of Dependency and Control—this Supreme Being with all its power, this God of Law with its commands of what must and must not be done, this God of Belief with its propositions about what must and must not be accepted as true—that the adolescing self both depends on and is controlled by. In the economy of the subject-object dichotomy, the adolescing self finds that the God of Dependency provides all the things that the adolescing self needs for its own growth and development, while the God of Control, with all of its immense power and authority, seems to leave little room to the adolescing self for any use of its own power and authority. The God of Dependency and Control is at once a God of Providence and a God of Domination. It is this latter God that Paul Tillich characterizes when he says, "God appears as the invincible tyrant, the being in contrast with whom all other beings are without freedom and subjectivity. He is equated with the recent tyrants who with the help of terror try to transform everything into a mere object, a thing among things, a cog in the machine they control."[14]

Ultimately, it seems, the issue with the God of Dependency and Control comes down to the question, who will write the script for my life? Is it God's life to sustain and to control, or is it my life? In actual fact, the God of Dependency and Control is already a contradiction. On the one hand, this God, who is all-powerful and all-knowing, offers its whole self for us and for our well-being; on the other hand, this God allows us no autonomy at all. On the one hand, this God appears to be calling us to more and more freedom and responsibility; on the other hand, this God seems to be demanding that we remain in a position of absolute dependence.

In its beginnings, the God of Dependency and Control often appears to be a wonderful and benignly protective parent, a God of Providence. Later, the adolescing self may come to experience this God more as an impersonal, uncaring power, a God of Domination. Throughout the whole time of its authority, however, the God of Dependency and Control promises to protect us from the pain of inner struggle and from having to make responsible life choices, on condition, of course, that we surrender any serious striving toward real freedom or autonomy. This promise of protection, which means that we are loved and cared for by God, is often enormously comforting and attractive to us. There may be ambivalent feelings, however, about this God of Dependency and Control—a God that offers protection at the price of freedom—and the individual may experience a great deal of conflict over who will have control over his or her life. In dealing with the God of Dependency and Control, the adolescing self may adopt a modus vivendi that goes back and forth on a continuum of gratitude, acceptance, questioning, and outright rebellion.

5. The Superego God is a God of the Group. The place where the Superego God lives, moves, and has its being is in the group. As described here, the God of the Group is, for all practical purposes, a gathering of adolescing selves around the all-powerful Supreme Being as its unseen center. The authority of the God of the Group lies with certain individuals who apparently are directly appointed for this task by the Supreme Being. Only those who have this authority can speak, and only those who have this authority can be heard. This authority makes clear to the group the dictates of the God of Law; this authority prescribes for the group the nature of the God of Belief; this authority sets forth the conditions of the God of Dependency and Control for being included or excluded from the group. The God of the Group is a powerful, hierarchical, and closed system. Only in and through the group can the adolescing self find how to know and to follow the Superego God.

The contradiction in the God of the Group lies essentially around the issue of belonging or not belonging, inclusion or exclusion, acceptance or nonacceptance. In the beginning, this God of the Group is often very loving, welcoming, nurturing, and affirming, and with this God, we can find wonderful solidarity, support, and strength. Later, however, the God of the Group may reveal itself as unbelievably heartless and uncaring, often leaving us feeling tremendous rejection and terrible isolation. The God of the Group is a God of Convention and a God of Conformity, and its scepter is a two-edged sword, at times seeming to have the power of life and death over us.

In its beginnings, the God of the Group appears as an extension of parental authority and care. Later, this God evolves into a corporate entity with clearly identifiable rules and an organizational structure. Throughout the whole time of its tenure, however, the God of the Group promises us safety and a divinely sanctioned place to belong— on condition that we are willing to adhere to the rules and precepts held by the group. This promise of safety is often enormously powerful and reassuring to us. Over time, however, we may develop ambivalent feelings about this God of the Group with its fixed moral laws, its set beliefs, and its demands of dependency and control. Considerable conflict may arise with this God. In dealing with this God, the adolescing self may find itself adopting a modus vivendi that goes back and forth among conforming to the God of the Group, rebelling against this God, and venturing away from this God on the basis of personal judgment and experience.

NOTES

1. Thomas Merton, "To Ripu Daman Lama," in *The Hidden Ground of Love: The Letters of Thomas Merton on Religious Experience and Social Concerns*, ed. William H. Shannon (New York: Farrar, Straus and Giroux, 1985), 452.

2. Paul Tillich, *The Courage to Be* (New Haven, CT: Yale University Press, 1952), 184. Himes, *Doing the Truth in Love*, 18, observes, "The notion of a supreme being belittles God. Calling someone or something the supreme being presumes that there is a class of things, beings, and that one of those beings is the number one being in the class, the supreme one."

3. Sigmund Freud, *The Future of an Illusion* (Garden City, NY: Anchor, 1964), 57.

4. Gordon D. Kaufman, "Mystery, Critical Consciousness, and Faith," in *The Rationality of Religious Belief*, ed. William J. Abraham and Steven W. Holtzer (Oxford: Clarendon, 1987), 56.

5. Nicholas P. Harvey, "Christian Morality and Pastoral Theology," in *The Blackwell Reader in Pastoral and Practical Theology*, ed. James Woodward and Stephen Pattison (Malden, MA: Blackwell, 2000), 190.

6. See Lawrence Kohlberg, *The Philosophy of Moral Development: Moral Stages and the Idea of Development* (San Francisco: Harper & Row, 1981).

7. David E. Schecter, "The Loving and Persecuting Superego," *Contemporary Psychoanalysis* 15, no. 3 (1979): 377.

8. John W. Glaser, "Conscience and Superego: A Key Distinction," in *Conscience: Theological and Psychological Perspectives*, ed. C. Ellis Nelson, 167–88 (New York: Newman, 1973), 177.

9. Maggie Ross, *Pillars of Flame: Power, Priesthood, and Spiritual Maturity* (San Francisco: Harper & Row, 1988), 117.

10. Freud, *Future of an Illusion*, 37.

11. Freud, *Future of an Illusion*, 76–77.

12. Mark C. Taylor, *Journeys to Selfhood: Hegel & Kierkegaard* (New York: Fordham University Press, 2000), 62.

13. Paul W. Pruyser, "Psychological Roots and Branches of Belief," *Pastoral Psychology* 28, no. 1 (Fall 1979): 11.

14. Tillich, *Courage to Be*, 185.

4

ADOLESCING RELIGION AND FORMAL RELIGION

Religion, as we have seen, is about "the self and God together." Religion, therefore, is relational and developmental. Adolescing religion—fettered as it is by fantasy, relating in transference, and the logic of objective knowing—is, of course, about the adolescing self and the Superego God together. At this point, we are in a position to describe the nature of adolescing religion in more detail by looking directly at the interaction of the self and God as it is in the early form of this "together." How does the adolescing self hear and communicate with the Superego God?

HEARING THE SUPEREGO GOD

The voice of the Superego God that the adolescing self hears is the all-powerful voice of the Supreme Being. It is the voice of the God of Law, commanding the self to do what is good and to avoid what is evil. It is the voice of the God of Belief, telling the adolescing self what he or she must believe in order to be acceptable. It is the voice of the God of Dependency and Control, on the one hand, establishing order and stability, and on the other hand, demanding that the adolescing self think and act in a number of circumscribed ways. And finally, it is the voice of the God of the Group, speaking to the adolescing self through the leaders of the group on whom authority has been conferred.

The voice of the Superego God is a voice that plays in the thoughts of the adolescing self. It is a parental voice that, however varying in tone, is often bent on having the adolescing self conform to the commands of the Superego God. Often this voice freezes the adolescing self in a sense of inadequacy, or guilt, or shame. Often this voice condemns the self for what it has done wrong or for what it is thinking of doing wrong. Often this voice is critical, harsh, and attacking, trying to get the adolescing self to see the error of its ways. Often this voice speaks with threatening, unassailable authority. And because this voice is so powerful and because it comes from such a distance, it may be a voice, as John Glaser notes, which comes to us as "cosmic, vast, and mysterious."[1] But distant or not, mysterious or not, often this voice is immediately there in our thinking. It tends to flood the head with ample measures of guilt along with dire scenarios and consequences, often before the adolescing self is able even to think its own thoughts.

Although we may not be aware of it, at least at first, often there is a great deal of contradiction to be heard in the voice of the Superego God. It is an external voice, but it is also an internal voice. It is not really my voice, but it also is my voice. It is a voice that appears to be concerned for me and to be in my best interest, but it also is a voice that belittles me and puts me down. It is a voice that seems to be quite rational, but it also is a voice that is often quite irrational as well.[2] The voice of the Superego God is, in fact, a still-forming, still-dependent voice, a fettered voice of ambiguity and of the different meanings others have found. Quite simply, the voice of the Superego God is a superego voice. It is a voice of external authority now internalized, a voice in the service of controlling—usually either through praise or through punishment—the still-forming, still-dependent adolescing self.

SPEAKING ABOUT AND TO THE SUPEREGO GOD

When speaking about the Superego God, the adolescing self uses terms that are apparently clear and objective. Reflecting the logic of objective knowing, our language about the Superego God is literal, that is, the words we use are presumed to have fixed, agreed upon, objective meanings. "Literal language," says June Singer, "is that in which words correspond exactly to objects, and the meaning conveyed by the words reflects the one-to-one correspondence."[3] There is a one-to-one correlation, therefore, between the words we use and the objectlike Supreme Being we represent with them. Moreover, the words mean what the adolescing self knows they mean, and apparently they mean what others mean when they use the same words. The Superego God is thought to be understood without ambiguity or confusion, because in a logic of objective knowing, the reality of God is contained in the meaning of the very words we use to speak of God. The words convey reality with black-and-white clarity; there is no gray.

It is possible to speak of the Superego God in literal terms, of course, because this Supreme Being is thought to be opposite the adolescing self in the closed world system of the subject-object split. Although this God is personal and parental, this God is also an object, and although as adolescing selves we are persons, we are also objectlike as well. At the superego level, our language about God reflects this inherent contradiction. Made confusing by fantasy, relating in transference, and the logic of objective knowing, our language about God is somehow personal and at the same time somehow literal and objective. "God is our father," for example, may be understood as personally descriptive and literally true. When the adolescing self speaks *about* the Superego God, the language often tends to be objective. There are facts to be known about the Superego God, and literal language is our way of capturing these facts. When the adolescing self speaks *to* the Superego God, that is, when we address the Superego God directly in prayer and petition, our language tends to be personal; we are, in fact, very much like children who are expressing their needs to their parents.

This description of adolescing religion is important for several reasons. First, it shows concretely how adolescing religion as the early relationship between the self and God is actually experienced and expressed. Second, it shows clearly the nature of the contradiction and the conflict that may arise between the adolescing self and the Superego God. Third, and perhaps most important, this description of adolescing religion is what religion is commonly understood to be. Although adolescing religion is only the early form of "the self and God together," it is, for all practical purposes, the normative understanding of religion that exists in society and in the culture.

FORMAL RELIGION

Although it may not be accurate to say that formal religion is the same thing as adolescing religion, it is important to observe that the structure of adolescing religion is usually what gives formal religion its distinctive character. If the voice we hear in adolescing religion is the voice of the Superego God, the voice we hear in formal religion is often the voice of the Superego God as well. The voice of adolescing religion is external; it comes from other people and from other sources outside of ourselves, and we are asked to internalize this voice, to take it inside and to make it our own. Likewise, the voice of formal religion is external and comes from other people and from sources outside of ourselves. It is the voice of the religious authority that we hear, and we are asked to take this voice inside and to make it our own. Formal religion is a voice of the God of the Group telling us who God is and how God must be understood and related to if we are to be a member of that religion.

In formal religion there are statements that describe the nature of God as the Supreme Being, and there are statements about the God of Law that tell the follower how he or she must act. There are statements about the God of Belief that tell the follower what he or she must adhere to, and there are statements that are meant to relate the follower to the God of Dependency and Control. And, of course, all these statements are made by the authorities who speak for the Superego God as the God of the Group. Moreover, in formal religion the meaning of all these statements is thought to be impersonal and objective.

"God is all just," for example, might be a statement of formal religion that is objective and literally true. But if, for example, you or I were to say, "You know, I don't find that God always acts justly at all," this kind of statement would have no place in formal religion. Objective meaning and formal religion go hand in hand, but personal meaning, which is the kind of meaning that we find in our own experience and the kind of meaning that becomes more and more important to us as we approach adulthood, has no necessary connection with formal religion at all. Although many people are able to find a great deal of personal meaning in formal religion, the validity of formal religion itself does not depend at all on anyone finding personal meaning in it. In formal religion, statements about God need not be verified by personal experience in order to be true.

If fantasy, relating in transference, and the logic of objective knowing are what inform adolescing religion, it might be expected that they would play a part in formal religion as well. Fantasy and relating in transference are handed down through the fettered imaging of those who have gone before us and can easily become part of the fabric of formal religion. We might want to trust the thinking of our ancestors, but as Freud cautions, "They believed in things we could not possible accept to-day; and the possibility occurs to us that the doctrines of religion may belong to that class too."[4]

The logic of objective knowing, along with its literal understanding of language, also comes into play. In fact, for many people the logic of objective knowing appears to be the very touchstone of what formal religion is. Rarely is formal religion understood as the collective experience of the faithful of a given place and time; the collective experience of those who have gone before us is not what gives it form. Rather, formal religion is presumed to be an impersonal and objective reality, a reality that we are able to capture in statements that are literally true. As Carl Jung reminds us, "Creeds are codified and dogmatized forms of original religious experience. The contents of the experience have become sanctified and usually congealed in a rigid, often elaborate, structure."[5] Dogma, he observes, "has become a tenet to be accepted in and for itself, with no basis in any experience that would demonstrate its truth."[6]

Just as there is a contradiction to be found in adolescing religion, there is usually a contradiction to be found in formal religion—at least in the way formal religion is commonly understood. On the one hand, statements about God may be the result of fantasy and relating in transference; on the other hand, these statements are supposed to be literally and objectively true. Often, however, this contradiction in formal religion is not so readily apparent. What comes from fantasy and from relating in transference in the teaching of the tradition tends to take on an objective quality with the passage of time. Therefore, what comes from the logic of objective knowing easily becomes the "form" of religion, and this logic is what allows us to understand religious statements as objectively and literally true.

NOTES

1. John W. Glaser, "Conscience and Superego: A Key Distinction," in *Conscience: Theological and Psychological Perspectives*, ed. C. Ellis Nelson, 167–88 (New York: Newman, 1973), 177.

2. For an excellent understanding of the voice of the superego and how to deal with this voice, see Eugene T. Gendlin, "A Process View of the Superego," in *Focusing-Oriented Psychotherapy: A Manual of the Experiential Method* (New York: Guilford, 1996), 247–58.

3. June Singer, *Seeing through the Visible World* (San Francisco: Harper & Row, 1990), 11.

4. Sigmund Freud, *The Future of an Illusion* (Garden City, NY: Anchor, 1964), 40.

5. Carl G. Jung, *Psychology and Religion* (New Haven, CT: Yale University Press, 1938), 6.

6. Carl G. Jung, *The Collected Works of C. G. Jung*, vol. 9, pt. 2, *Aion: Researches into the Phenomenology of the Self* (Princeton, NJ: Princeton University Press, 1979), 178.

5

IMAGES OF THE
SUPEREGO GOD

This chapter on images of the Superego God presents the stories of
a number of people I interviewed over the past few years. All of
the people who are included in this chapter are chronological adults
over the age of twenty-five. In conducting these interviews, my primary
objective was to allow each of the interviewees to say as clearly as he or
she could just how it was that they presently imaged God. Often I began with the question, if you had to say right now how you image God
in your life, what would that image be like? And I would usually add,
"I am not so much interested in what you think about God or what you
know about God. I am interested in your present image of God. What
is God like for you right now?" The interview would unfold from there.
I was also interested in anything the interviewees saw as a change in
their imaging of God as adulthood unfolded or in anything they saw as
different from the imaging of God they had as a child.

Each of these interviews was taped. I had a number of questions that
covered all the characteristics of God that are included in the theoreti-
cal parts of this book, questions, for example, about faith, about morality, and about dependency and control. I also asked the interviewees
about their personal experiences of God, about experiences of church
or organized religion, and about what prayer and their relationship
with God was like. However, I did not have a uniform set of questions
that I asked everyone. Rather, I tried to let the narrative unfold as naturally as possible. Often, I would say to the interviewee, "I am trying to

get as clear a picture as possible of who God is for you. I only want to know who God is for you." And I would go where the person wanted to go. I did not want those I interviewed to answer my questions so much as to tell their stories of God. To that end, in fact, I present the images of God in this chapter in narrative form rather than in interview form. Each person's story represents his or her unique picture of God.

All of the stories in this chapter are meant to demonstrate the paradigm of "the Superego God." My hope is that as they are told, they can interact with the theory in such a way that they make the theory more understandable and more real, even as the theory may help to make the stories more understandable and more real. These stories are not meant, however, to be representative of all the different versions of the Superego God. Nor are most of these stories about a Superego God in its purest form. All of these stories have definite elements of the Superego God, but there is in some of them—as might be expected—movement toward a Living God as well. As we will see, some of these stories go directly back to childhood because the roots of the Superego God are there. They are told here because, for the teller of the story, they are, or at least they were, very much alive in chronological adulthood.

While it is fair to say that all of the stories in this chapter are about experiences of God, it is also fair to say that there is not much mutual relating in them. All of them show, for the most part, a "distanced," as opposed to a "close," relationship with God. Many of these stories shared by the interviewees are, in fact, very painful. They are often stories of fear, guilt, judgment, disillusion, confusion, anger, and rejection. A harsh and critical Superego God is in these stories. A God of fettered imaging is in these stories. The Supreme Being, the God of Law, the God of Belief, the God of Dependency and Control, and the God of the Group is in these stories.

IMAGES OF GOD

Alice

Alice is a single woman in her thirties who was raised in a strict but loving family. After working for several years as a secretary, she went back to school to become a social worker. In the community agency she now works for, she is seen as very competent and as very dedicated to her clients. We will hear from Alice again in chapter 14, because her imaging of God started to become transformed in her later twenties. Until that time, however, she lived, or she attempted to live, with a fearful image of God that she had from the time she started grade school.

I just remember being incredibly afraid. I was a scaredy cat as a kid, so the first day of school, I was terrified. Hell was mentioned a lot, and I didn't want to go there. So I was going to learn everything and conform to any religious person. First grade, I'm going to be a nun. That was it. I was going to be a nun. My mom wanted to be a nun, but she had four kids and she got married, so that was out. So, you know, my mom being that way and seeing the nuns who know all that stuff and are very close to God, then if I'm one of them, I'm okay. I was six or seven then.

I went to church a lot when I was young, but I don't know if that wasn't just a conformist route to take. I don't know how much of that has to do with what you can do at seven and eight and nine years old. I don't know what your potential is to understand God in the abstract. God was just someone so far above us, that you could know about, that you could answer on a test. You know, no sense of intimacy or a father. God was someone very authoritarian, you know, just waiting for you to make a mistake, and then you get a punishment. Just like a punishing kind of God. It was fear, big time fear, and it stayed with me for a very long time.

A punishing kind of God, that was the way it was. Never really, you know, never really relaxed. Never feel good enough, never feel like you are doing it right, waiting for the other shoe to drop. The closest thing is like your parents, because you need it concrete when you're a kid, obeying your parents, being good in class, being selfless as much as you know how at that age, not fighting, not getting angry. Getting angry in our house was a big thing when we were growing up. It's not like my parents were terrible people. They weren't. They were very kind and patient with us kids. But I ended up with a lot of fear about God. It certainly wasn't healthy. It was a pseudorelationship. I could never be secure. I could never be myself. I could never relax.

Marty

Marty, a serious and thoughtful single man in his early thirties, has been working most recently in a residential program for troubled teenagers. Marty had an early experience of organized religion as external control, which is still very much with him. There is a sense in him that if religion were to be real, it would have to be something very personal and private. Inside there may be some connection with God, but it would be betrayed if manifested in words or in outward signs.

I remember how I was taught to pray. It was all external. You were required to learn these prayers, and, you know, the meaning of prayer was never discussed. And it didn't take into account your own truth. Just last week, I took my two-year-old niece for a walk to the park. I enjoyed just watching her. There was something very sweet and innocent about it. And there was no agenda on my part. I am watching this innocent child being curious, and I am enjoying it immensely. There is nothing she had to do, and there was nothing that I wanted her to do. Maybe that's what divine presence means. But it's not what happens in church. In church, it is all about control.

There's something about beliefs. I'm sure a lot of that stuff has a lot of value, a lot of beauty, and a lot of validity. But the inclination on my part is always to distrust anything that is said from the outside, anything read from the outside, because, you know, it's just somebody ready to spout the party line, just somebody trying to control me and get me to do something. I don't trust religious people, because they have a hidden agenda. They might seem very nice, but sooner or later they are going to tell you what you have to do.

Patty

After one of the workshops I gave on "The Superego God and the Living God," Patty, a single mother with two young children, wrote me a letter, sharing her sense of the Superego God in some personal reflections and in a poem. In the workshop, Patty had said rather poignantly that her God—which she saw as a fear-evoking and punitive Superego God—was no longer real or meaningful for her. She longed for something more in God, but she was not able to find it.

My Superego God is someone I'm afraid of. I learned as a child that God punishes wrongdoing. I've internalized this God as someone who is always watching me, who knows what I'm doing. I experience Him as controlling, as someone who is all-good, but on His terms.

I think of my Superego God, and I think of limitations. I think of praying and asking for protection. But for things to be well in my life and for those prayers to be answered, it necessitates being good, obeying the rules as I learned as a child. I don't pray now nearly as much as I used to. My Superego God doesn't make sense to me like He used to, and I haven't any real replacement—there's a void, a vacuum in His place.

My Superego God is still, however, inside my head. He is a God of the head and not of the heart. I don't have a relationship with Him. There's no emotional investment. He is a God of rules, a God of the church, almighty, omnipotent, and distant. A wondrous God to be feared, respected, and assuaged. A God, I feel, of "the few," interpreted by "the select." And in seeing Him thus, I realize God must surely be above and beyond this narrowness, these limitations. God, I feel, is bigger by far than the way I learned about Him, but I have no route at present to develop any closer link or understanding.

My Superego God
My Superego God clings on tightly,
His might is weak, His hold a fragile bind.
Know Me for what I tell you,
Not for what you feel and what I am.
The inheritance of moral rules and regulations,
Imprison, confine, and define,
Leaving souls in chains or wandering and wasting.
All at sea, lost in different places,
Finding temporary oasis in translation or rejection,
Of their God of presentation.
Body alive, body dead, no tangible difference,
The enormity of what's missing continues today.
But the God that can't be seen is witnessed,
In the life force, in the felt sense, in the interim
Between the concrete and illusion.

Superego God, you've lost your inheritance.
Your claim is being slowly denied.
Experienced truths find greatest favor,
Hereditary privilege is destroyed.
God is strongest, not in laws,
But in the sublime.

Elizabeth

Elizabeth has been a high school teacher for many years. She had a long struggle with a very serious form of cancer in midlife. But until that time—really up until she was in her forties—she suffered from a scrupulosity that crippled her sense of herself and crippled her relationship with God. A widow with two grown children, Elizabeth is a very generous person who is committed to the students she works with in an inner-city high school. We will pick up Elizabeth's story again in chapter 14, but the beginnings of her story are here.

I don't know if I remember an early image of God. I just remember the distinct point where my faith went from a complete childlike aspect to a rules relationship with God. At the age of seven, I became very rules conscious. At a time when it should have been a happy time, it became a time of me thinking of God as this person that has these rules and these regulations. I was always looking for the right rule. And that followed me right through life. There was something that made a complete reversal of childlike trust. I was always scared that I was doing the wrong thing. So that's the kind of image I have had of God.

Before I was seven, I considered myself normal. Normal in the sense that I don't remember having any problems with the scrupulosity I have had all these years. Grade school was about all these rules, rules for this, rules for that. "These are the rules, and if you don't obey them, you're gonna be punished." God was the law and the rule, and if you didn't follow it, you're guilty and you're sinful. The whole thing worked on you so. I was guilty all the time. I was racked with guilt for years. Like a cult thing, I think. I was brought up almost in a cult, because I believed it all. I took it all in. Others didn't, but I did. I was afraid all the time, afraid to do anything wrong. It was very, very sad.

See, my mother was a scrupulous, perfectionistic kind of person. I blame the church, but I think my mother had a lot to do with it. So it's a personality trait that's in the family. Sort of a scrupulosity and a perfectionism. I see it in my sisters, and I see it in my mother. So, the church telling me these rules was, to a person that had that kind of streak anyway, well, it took on me. There were all those things that I was told that I had to believe, and I just accepted them and believed them. I didn't even question them or what they meant. I was afraid to think for myself. Even when I knew what was right, I would always have to have somebody in authority say it was right. I don't think I ever lost that. It was horrible. I mean, that I couldn't enjoy my life.

Now, as I'm thinking about it, a father image probably would have been what I remember, too, like an image of a trusting father. The Good Shepherd comes to my mind. You know, somebody-taking-care-of-His-flock kind of thing. Yeah, and I was the child and He was the father. But I think that was in the background, a background image. But in front was the rules thing that kept me from really realizing that the background person was there. I mean, that God would be there to show me what I needed to do, that I would have a more trusting attitude instead of ending up with so much fear.

Michael

Michael is a successful businessman now living in the United States, his adopted country. A gay man in midlife, he is courageously trying to sort out the pieces of his life. After many years of anguish and personal devastation, he is struggling to make all the parts of himself fit into some kind of living whole. Michael also attended a workshop I offered on "The Superego God and the Living God." I asked him if he would write down some of the experience of the Superego God he shared in the workshop—profound experiences of rejection, shame, and guilt. He sent me the following reflection.

The description of the Superego God was everything that I knew. For me, God, the Superego God, meant fear, shame, guilt, exclusion, a sense of being unacceptable, a sense of unworthiness, and an overwhelming sense of being judged. I grew up in a dysfunctional family, in a country torn by religious divisions. The Superego God was used mainly as a weapon to control, and at the same time, we were told that our God was superior to the God of the "others." All of this left me very confused.

As I struggled with my identity as a gay man, the message I received (from the Superego God) was one of rejection, shame, and guilt. The people who controlled the spreading of this message (the church) told me I did not belong, leaving me confused, isolated, and suicidal. The Superego God told me I was not to question, but I was to accept all I was taught. The Superego God kept me in a state of fear and panic as I suffered in silence from an overwhelming anxiety based on the guilt within, that if I was to become the person I knew I was, then I was damned. Later, that same God caused me so much guilt about my own financial success, that I thought that to have money or success was to be moving in the opposite direction from God.

As I searched for comfort from this harsh Superego God, I found relief to some degree from alcohol. I could numb the feelings of self-hatred and that awful sense that I was unlovable, unlovable not only to myself but most certainly to the Superego God. This God led me to the pits of despair and self-mutilation. It kept me locked in a world of deceit and darkness, and ultimately it brought me to the inside of mental institutions. It was in one of those mental institutions that I was introduced to the "twelve step recovery program" of Alcoholics Anonymous (AA). It was in this program that I learned that if I was going to recover, I had to face the Superego God and challenge all that I had been taught. In fact, if I was to become free of the self-destructive path I was on, I had to smash the concept of the Superego God entirely.

I have been in recovery for more than a year now. With the help of counseling, I am starting to value myself as a person and to claim my life as my own.

Harry

Harry is a man who was raised in no particular religious tradition. He is a single man in midlife, and several months ago he entered a court-ordered rehabilitation program for addiction to drugs. Until recently, he sensed that his life was "kind of empty," that he was just passing through life without much sense of anything that was important and without much connection with other people. I asked Harry who God was for him, and it was a question he found himself thinking about more seriously.

God is a good, orderly director. It is more like nature, the natural flow of things, a force, or a spirit of the universe, or a flow that keeps things going. God is the way it all works. The sun comes up, the sun comes down. It's the flow, the order of things working together. It works with the universe, and it works with individuals as well, because the flow does not want anything bad to happen. It is for the good, for going in the right direction. Sometimes God puts people in your life when you need them. We can still make choices, but the good is there for healing.

I am praying now since I've been in rehab, and I feel protected by God. I ask for what I need. I say, "You have to help me." If I really want something, I pray, and then usually it comes the way I need it to come. But what comes is to help us to grow.

Edward

Edward, a man with an engineering background who is very successful, works in the area of information technology. He is in his middle thirties, married, and has three young children. He is a serious man and a careful thinker. Questions of meaning and questions of personal responsibility are the most important questions in his life. When I asked Edward how he imaged God, he responded very clearly, but with a conflict in his imaging of God that was quite pronounced.

The one thing I had as a child and that persists today is that I have always had a very strong dichotomy between God the Father and God the Son. I have two images of God. I believe they are the same God, but they are very different images. I believe they are two faces of the same God, two expressions of the same God. God the Father I have had a difficult time imaging and a difficult time relating to. God the Son has always been an image or a person that I have been more comfortable with. When I have negative thoughts about my religion, they are usually aimed toward God the Father. When I experience positive thoughts, they are usually attributed to my vision of Jesus, God the Son.

God the Father, which I associate with the Old Testament, is a very distant figure for me. It's not a being I have an easy time relating to. I don't even know if I can picture God the Father. When I picture God the Father, I picture sort of a great expanse of space. I picture, you know, the earth, the stars, the sun, and sort of this overarching force of good in the world. But I don't have a very clear picture of what God the Father is.

God the Father is scary. I was scared to death of God as a kid, and I'm still scared to death of this God. I don't get a lot of positive guidance from God the Father. There are a lot of negative principles in this God. There's no image there I can relate to. I keep this God out of my mind. I try to isolate it. I usually think about God the Father when I feel guilty about something. And then I think, "God! I am going to go to hell." I only think of this image of God when I'm in a sort of negative frame of mind.

God the Son is a face of God I can relate to. My image of God the Son is what you would see in many of the Renaissance paintings of Christ. It's a Christ that looks like you and me, but also a Christ that is, in expression and temperament, sort of above the human condition, somebody who is all-loving, all-seeing, and very kind. His conduct is generally not dictated by emotions. He is a beneficial individual. It's the view of what you might see depicted by Michelangelo.

God the Son is generally more compassionate than God the Father and more interested in the day-to-day lives of human beings like myself. I think God the Son wants us to live good, moral lives, and He is interested in what it takes to accomplish that. He is a God involved in our existence. God the Son has more influence on me. He allows me to guide my life with principles I can relate to. I've never questioned whether there is a God. My faith is a very deep-rooted belief in the principles of God the Son. I believe in all the "thou shalt nots" of the Ten Commandments, but in terms of a positive moral philosophy that I can live by, I believe in the principles of the New Testament. I believe in God the Son, the kindness, the compassion, the love. Love is a very conscious effort to do something which is good from a moral standpoint. That's a very radical thought. That's the kind of love of God the Son.

I give some weight to what the church says, but in my own personal life, I don't give it overwhelming weight. It would never make my decision for me. In making my decisions, I look to the principles of God the Son. I look to the New Testament. Maybe it's my education, but there is a philosophical grounding in the New Testament, there is a way of life in the New Testament that I have never been able to find anywhere else.

The world is God's crucible. We are put into it, and through the fires of life, all its trials and tribulations, stuff is either burned off, and we are made more pure, and more hearty, and more righteous, or through that fire, the matter of your soul is made corrupt, and we never become part of the spirit of righteousness and goodness which is God. The experience of life to me is sort of like a testing ground. It's my life. I get to do whatever I want, sink or swim. It's my decision. Although I think God the Son is a kind of "hands on" God, you know, a kind, compassionate God, I also think He's a "hands off" God—not quite as much as God the Father, who only comes in when something really bad happens, and then He smites everyone. But God the Son will allow us the rope we need either to build something or to hang ourselves. And it's really our call. There's a lot of freedom there. This God lets us be free.

This notion of freedom as a core personal principle is something that came to me in my late twenties. I was doing a lot of personal reflection. I studied Beethoven, and I was very influenced by his life. He helped me figure it all out. Here was a man who was abused as a child by his father, went out to work as a musician, and then started becoming deaf. He has this terrible situation, and the way he confronts it is by fighting through it and never losing his faith. And with all his difficulties and with terrible health problems, he wrote one of the most beautiful pieces of music, an inspiring piece of music with very strong religious undertones, the Ninth Symphony. And he's deaf. That put it all together for me. It said to me that adversity isn't a bad thing. It's how you react to it that defines you, that just because you are under tough circumstances, you don't have to lose your faith in God. From that, I began to understand freedom in a personal sense. And then my image of God changed dramatically at that point.

I don't think God wants us praying about some of the material things that don't matter. All that does is tell God you still haven't got it yet. I think that God wants us praying about the deeper questions. For example, how do you balance being a member of modern society with the need to be charitable? I live now in an environment that encourages self-indulgence. It's all about me, and my career, and my goals. I should be thinking more about doing the right thing and about how I can help others. That's something I struggle with. The dynamic between God and me has matured. God is saying, "You know Ed, you're on this planet, you know what you gotta do. Call me when you need me. But you've got the ball." It's "hands off." It's how I respond that is important.

There will be a reckoning. I don't know when it will be. I've had all this freedom. What have I done with it? There have been times when I've reacted well, where my soul benefited, but there have been plenty of times where I've reacted poorly, knowing that it was a poor reaction. I believe that God forgives, but I believe that the contrition that needs to be felt has a very high standard. It needs to be born of a great deal of conscious suffering, that you need to be aware that you were bad. I think when you expire, your soul needs to be in a certain state. I have a road map. I know I need to follow it, but I don't know what's coming at the end of the road. Where it ends up is a mystery.

I tend to see things in black and white, too categorical, maybe. The separation I have between God the Son and God the Father is probably an artifice. It allows me to have my religion and still stay sane. Otherwise, I'd be lost. There are really two sides to God, one I'm not comfortable with, and one I am comfortable with. How do you blend those two visions? Because, as I see it now, it's not the case that God is that way. I just sort of use this way of seeing it for myself. At this point, I don't know how they intersect. God the Father is a fearsome entity. He can do some pretty bad stuff. He could smite me like that. He isn't a safe being. I need to feel like the universe is a good place, but I can't with God the Father. With God the Son, you can just keep trying; you can get a second chance. I need to find a way to combine those two views into a vision which is whole.

I have a fear that my image of God the Son is sort of fanciful. It may be all about God the Father. And in which case, I'm screwed. God's conduct has not been consistent over time. God the Father is no-nonsense. See, maybe I'm giving God the Son too much credit in terms of being for-

giving and kind. For a very long time, there was God the Father, and He was a pretty tough character. And now, for a fraction of that time, we have sort of seen a new side of God. I hope that lasts. I'm not sure the New Testament God is here to stay. Maybe God the Father is more in control. Maybe He will have the final say. It's true. I really do have a dichotomy in how I image God. I have two very distinct images of God, and they are very different. I don't know how they interact. I don't know for myself how to blend the two into a sort of global view of what this is.

Seymour

A single man in his middle twenties, Seymour comes from a country in the southern part of Africa. Educated both in Great Britain and in Canada, he has always been attracted to working with people who are on the margins of society or who are disadvantaged in some way. For the past year, he has been working for a homeless shelter run by a religious group. Soft-spoken, articulate, and quite sensitive to loss, he was very open in sharing his images of who God is for him. Much like Edward, he has images of a harsh God and a loving God that are at war with each other.

Right now I feel like God is the ultimate unknown. Right now I feel that even trying to get any definition of God is kind of inadequate. I have a lot of ideas about God, but I don't feel I can put my full trust in any of them. The image of God that I would like to believe in the most is God as a loving person—a father or mother figure—but I don't feel that that completely describes who God is. My image of God underwent a pretty dramatic change when my mother actually was murdered by my step-father when I was away in secondary school. When that happened, I felt that the image of the loving, personal, caring God was incomplete, and I felt that there was another side of God I did not know.

At first I was angry. How could this loving God let this happen to me? And over time, I felt it wasn't right to blame God. I started out with an image of God that was incomplete. This experience taught me another side of God which I do not know, which I am not aware of, which I cannot comprehend fully as a finite human being. I am at the point where I cannot say I believe in God, and I cannot say that I don't believe in God. Both of those statements feel absurd. I cannot have the confidence to say I don't believe in God. That to me would be extremely arrogant. But at the same time, I do want to believe in God, and I kind of have an intuitive sense that there is a God. Having been humbled by this experience, I feel I cannot understand who God is. I don't trust myself enough to make any definite pronouncements about who God is.

I have a lot of different images of God, but I can't honestly say I can put faith in each single image. The two great warring images that I have are the loving God I was raised to believe in and . . . I need to modify this. Actually there are not two images but three images. There's the loving God on the one end, and then there's a kind of impersonal God, a force that is not particularly concerned with the events of the individual per se, and then there's sort of the almost primitive sort of judging, judgmental, angry God, who is just very harsh with humans and who does care about humans personally, but from a very judgmental standpoint. This is the type of God who will write down how many sins you have done every single day. This is kind of the shadow image of God that I think we all have, that God is counting up your sins. It's one of the images I think of when I think of God, but it's not a very conscious image. It's not a very prevalent image, but every once in a while, it's there.

This harsh image of God comes out especially in some of my dreams. I've noticed that every once in a while I get these powerful dreams that point to how guilty I feel about not having remained faithful in an orthodox image of God. Occasionally, I have dreams even of going to hell or being punished because I have strayed from the path. I feel that that image of God manifests itself in some of my nightmares, but I don't really put faith in that image of God. But I acknowledge that it's part of my concept of God, that there is sort of a darker side to my images of God. All my images of God come to me in my dreams, from the loving, caring God, who is there and who is comforting, even when I'm sad and lonely, to the other side, to the other God, who is more judgmental and who tells me I have strayed from my path and that I'm not following His will. I don't think any of these images is God. It's just part of my struggle with God and with who I am.

One of the things that actually makes me uncomfortable with a lot of organized religion generally is the way a lot of people use God as a way to just project their own ego and project their own kind of power into the world. When I hear politicians say that they get their counsel from God for what they're doing, to me that is extremely blasphemous. To use the name of all that is good and perfect and holy in the world to promote policies that I feel—that if there was a God—would just be completely contrary to what God would really want. I feel kind of repulsed by that comfort level of just being able to say, "Well, I get my direction from God, and He tells me to do this or that." It's so simplistic and appalling to say, for example, "Well, our country is good, and everyone else is bad." From politicians, and from evangelists who are a little shady, I get the sense they are not taking the turn to God seriously enough, that they are just using God to promote themselves.

I don't think the problem is organized religion per se. I have a lot of very close friends who I believe are spiritual in the way you are meant to be spiritual. For them it's a constant struggle. It's a constant searching. It's a constant desire to grow closer to that deeper part of themselves. That's the type of spirituality that I respect and that is very often found in people who are part of organized religion. But there is also that other side, and Jesus was talking about this all the time. There are the people who claim that they know God because they obey certain strict rules or guidelines. "See, because I've done this and this and this, I know God, and I am holy. Therefore, I get to judge everyone else." And I guess it's that part of organized religion I am leery of. I guess that comes directly from their image of God, that there is a God up there who has a scorecard.

No one fits into a box. The mystery of God is part of the mystery of the self. You don't ever know yourself fully, just as I think God is always a mystery—a path, and a struggle, and a way, rather than an end in and of itself. Now I understand it's not just about questions and answers. I feel that contradiction is just part of the human experience, and what is attractive about the God concept is that you hope that in the end, even though you don't understand it as an individual, that there is a greater purpose and framework and that it all makes sense. But at the individual level, it often doesn't seem to make sense. I am only barely beginning to understand that what happened to me years ago might possibly have a meaning in terms of who I am now.

I want to say I believe in God. I want to have faith. I want to feel that everything has a purpose, but I can't. If I said that I believed in God, I would be a little bit like a hypocrite, like it's not completely how I feel. But at the same time, I still think of God as the most sacred thing that there is. I almost guard that thing very jealously in the sense that it's my own little secret, that I like God, but from a distance. Now, the question for me is, what does the presence of God mean? I've never really come to terms with that. What does it mean that God loves you? What does it mean that God cares about you? Life can be really harsh to very good people. If God loves you and God is present, how does that affect your life? And I don't know. I don't need a cerebral answer. I need an experiential answer.

I don't get a sense of any presence there. I get a sense of great, mysterious aloofness. And not necessarily a judging, condemnatory aloofness. But it's like I am this speck, and God is way up there, and He is so "other." So what does it mean to have a personal relationship with something that's so beyond you? That's my problem with saying I have faith. I pray, and it brings me some peace. But I don't understand it at all. I guess it's a question of trust, and I am not comfortable with that. From my family, there is this sense of loneliness and abandonment, and when I think about God, I guess that carries over as well.

II

THE LIVING GOD

6

THE ADULT SELF

It is hard to know with accuracy when anyone is functioning as an adult. Becoming an adult self is a human, interpersonal realization that happens gradually over time, and it may not be a "once and for all" occurrence. When the adult self is being realized, however, I believe it is important to value this realization for what it actually is, the transformation of the adolescing self into a new and wonderful level of human being that is qualitatively and functionally full and complete.[1] Quite simply, human adulthood is the major developmental achievement of life. It is the fullness of what it means to be human. Moreover, it is a passage into maturity, which for many of us is claimed only after long and painful personal struggle. In fact, it seems that there is much in contemporary culture that encourages a denial of adulthood, creating a problem as real and certainly as damaging to personal and interpersonal development as the widely recognized denial of death.[2]

The adult self is simply defined as an *integral self-in-mutuality*.[3] No longer still-forming and still-dependent, the adult self is now an undivided, integral whole. This self is "a single whole system,"[4] a cohesive gestalt in which all the parts function for the good of the whole. As "a consistent and coherent sense of personal identity,"[5] as "a unity, a continuity and a mastery in the midst of the confusion of immediate experience,"[6] this self has the strength and courage to be its own center within its own boundaries. Carl Jung calls this adult self a "psychic whole that is capable of resistance and abounding in energy."[7] Clifford Geertz's understanding of the person in the West as in part "a dynamic center of awareness, emotion, judgment, and action organized into a distinctive whole" is a good description of the adult self.[8] Even if it has some flaws and defects, the adult self is its own "whole."[9] It may not be a perfect whole, but it is an integrated and functioning whole, a whole that can continue to develop as itself.

At the same time, no longer still-forming and still-dependent, an adult self as its own functioning whole now relates in mutuality to what is other than itself. The adult self is necessarily a self-in-relatedness.[10] "The human person," as John McDargh insists, "is born with a *primary and irreducible need for the confirmation and affirmation of relationship.*"[11] From the very beginning of life, "mutuality enables the self to be what it is and become what it is becoming."[12] As the self reaches adulthood, the integrity of the self is realized only in mutual relating with others whose integrity is also recognized and respected. The dynamic of this relating lies in Gabriel Marcel's thinking, "others give me to myself."[13] The paradox of this relating lies in Paul Ricoeur's notion that there is "no other-than-the-self without a self."[14] The adult self continues to transform itself and continues to develop in integrity through the mutuality of relating. Without real dialogue and without mutual relationships of solicitude, love, respect, and understanding, the adult self simply cannot continue to be itself.[15]

"Crucial to a mature sense of mutuality," observes Judith Jordan, "is an appreciation of the wholeness of the other person, with a special awareness of the other's subjective experience."[16] In adult relating in mutuality, the distinctness and the integrity of each person is experienced, along with the needs, the values, and the unique concerns of each person.[17] In adult relating in mutuality, our basic moral attitude is one of care and justice for each person. In adult relating in mutuality, the interaction we have with each other—and with whatever else commands our response—is characterized by an attitude of honesty, openness, and concern. In adult relating in mutuality, our experience is one of trust and love toward the other and a willingness to let the other change as the relationship unfolds. In adult relating in mutuality, our ability to give and to receive what we need fosters the ongoing growth and development of each person. In an adult relating in mutuality, there is, therefore, a "common flourishing of all parties involved."[18]

As an integral self-in-mutuality, an adult self is, of course, a transformation of the still-forming and still-dependent adolescing self. Not only is the adolescing self transformed into a self that is integral and able to relate in mutuality, but the adult self that emerges from this transformation is now both a *process* and a *paradox*.[19] As its own functioning whole, the adult self is a process because it is able to continue to develop as its own self in full mutuality with what is other. "Process means that the self is a living whole with inner workings integrated enough to allow it to move and grow as itself in interaction with other selves."[20] As its own functioning whole, the adult self is a paradox because some significant ways this self "is" and "is not" are able to live together in an evolving unity of creative tension. "Paradox in adulthood basically means that the dichotomies, the contradictions, and the differences in the self and its way of relating are able to exist together."[21]

As the adolescing self is transformed into the process and the paradox of adulthood, the two major dichotomies that have characterized the experience of an adolescing self, the mind-body dichotomy and the subject-object dichotomy, are also transformed, at least in principle. The mind-body dichotomy, which Carl Rogers addresses, is an "inner" dichotomy. It splits the self from itself, leaving the self divided. The subject-object dichotomy, which is essential to the logic of objective knowing, is an "outer" dichotomy. It splits the self from what is other, leaving our reality divided. As these two major dichotomies, which function together in an adolescing self, are healed and transformed, how we have our experience is also healed and transformed. An adult self—and only an adult self—is able to have its experience in some wholeness. Experience is no longer dichotomized, no longer split. That is why the experience of an adult self is the experience of an integral self-in-mutuality.

With the transformation of the mind-body and the subject-object dichotomies, a number of other dichotomies that characterize thinking in adolescing religion can be healed and transcended as well: the self and God, the human and the religious, nature and God, body and soul, good and evil, masculine and feminine, the past and the present, temporal and eternal, the material and the spiritual, the sacred and the secular, the natural and the supernatural, faith and reason, reason and emotion, language and experience, psychology and religion, science and religion. The adult self and dichotomies do not go together.

SIX CHARACTERISTICS OF THE ADULT SELF

There are a number of characteristics important for a fuller understanding of the adult self as an integral self-in-mutuality. In the interest of clarity, these characteristics are presented here in six predicates, each one a substantive quality of the adult self and reflecting the process and the paradox of this self.

1. The adult self *is a body-self.*
2. The adult self *is founded in feeling.*
3. The adult self *has a sense of depth.*
4. The adult self *has clear boundaries.*
5. The adult self *exists in intimacy.*
6. The adult self *is its own responsible process.*

1. The primary characteristic of the adult self is that it is a body-self. The adult self is an embodied self; it is "a self that finds its anchor in its own body."[22] What this means is that the body is owned by the self, and the self is comfortable in the body. Self and body are united. When the self has become adult, the body is no longer something it *has*; the body is what it *is*. As Marcel says so simply, "I *am* my body."[23] To experience the self is to be at home in the body, and to be at home in the body with its own unique ways of being and with its own memories, desires, and limits is to experience the self.

This adult self is, as Rogers would describe it, a self which is "aware of" and "in harmony with" the experiencing of its whole body.[24] In other words, the self and the body—or if you will, "the mind" and the body—are now one in a way that was not possible before.[25] It is this integrity of the body-self that allows for the paradox that at times the body is present to us, making us very aware that we are embodied selves, and at other times, for example, when we are fully involved in something, the body is absent, as if it were not there at all.[26] It is also this integrity of the body-self that allows for comfort and trust in the self even as it makes mature affective relationships and commitments possible.[27]

"Being a body defines the nature and structure of our experience."[28] Marcel, who can be thought of as a philosopher of the adult self, describes various modes of being, such as fidelity, hope, love, and communion, as embodied realities.[29] And, of course, Freud's famous dictum "to love and to work" can easily be seen as presupposing the wholeness of an adult body-self. Although our culture has long harbored a "suspicion of embodiment,"[30] the truth is that only in and through the body-self are we fully ourselves and fully able to engage what is other, making real community possible. Only in and through the body-self are we an integral self-in-mutuality.

2. The adult self is founded in feeling. Feeling is the felt, meaningful aliveness of the body-self and the sense of this self in relatedness. "As a self, I am a subject or center of feeling, weaving together many different strands of relatedness into my identity."[31] "Once the capacity to feel is gone," observes Michael Hardiman, "then the person as a unique identity is lost."[32] Wilson Van Dusen calls feeling "the background accompaniment of all perception, all thought, all action."[33] James Nelson brings out the relatedness of feeling when he defines it as "the wholeness of the human response to reality."[34] Marcel makes the connection between feeling and the body clear with his assertion that it is "the act of feeling which is at the root of the affirmation *I am my body* and is its necessary foundation."[35] And David Levin observes that "our capacity to develop as human beings in the fullest sense depends upon our capacity to develop a felt sense of the body as a whole."[36] It is in the intimacy of feeling that the body-self is available to itself, and it is in the intimacy of feeling that the body-self is open to others and to the world, making real community possible.

Feeling, which is a unity of emotion and cognition, "refuses to submit," says Edward Casey, "to the dichotomies so obsessively pursued by reason."[37] John Heron observes, "Feeling is deeply and deliciously paradoxical. It unites us with what is other while telling us that it is other and that we are other to it. It celebrates unity in diversity, identification with what is different without loss of personal distinctness."[38] For Rogers, of course, the adult or congruent self is really a process of bodily felt interaction,[39] a process that he also understands as both cognitive and affective.[40] This process of bodily felt interaction is a locus, says Eugene Gendlin, of "felt meaning," which can be made explicit.[41] The ability to express feeling both reveals and evokes the adult self as an integral self-in-mutuality.

3. *The adult self has a sense of depth.* Living in the fullness of the body, there is a "pervasive inner sense of self."[42] "We are," says Charles Taylor, "creatures with inner depths; with partly unexplored and dark interiors."[43] Augusto Blasi speaks of "deep, preconscious feelings of rootedness and well-being, self-esteem, and purposefulness."[44] William Meissner notes "an inner feeling of worth, trustworthiness, autonomy, and capability."[45] Ira Progoff describes the "feeling of a creative power working within."[46] In the religious tradition, this depth is often understood as "interiority" or the "inwardness" of the person. Some see this depth as the place of "soul" because the essence of the human is there.[47] Some call this depth the "heart" because it is a living center of striving and courage.[48] Some understand this depth as the locus of the "spirit" because aliveness, purpose, and resolve are celebrated there.[49] All that is most personal to the adult self is both revealed and concealed in the depth.

Depth for an adult self as an integral self-in-mutuality means that there is something "more" in who I am, and it also means that there is something "more" in what is other. I can sense this "more" in its intuitions and in its inspirations, its desires and its secrets, its memories and its mysteries.[50] The depth is really the place of felt connection to myself and to what is other than myself, allowing for more extensive identifications, more profound meanings, and a deeper sense of both integrity and compassion. This depth is a paradox; in it we are uniquely different from one another, yet somehow very much the same, and we are profoundly alone, yet intimately bonded together. The depth is a place "where I experience the other in myself and the other-than-myself experiences me."[51] Living in the body allows for an owned sense of depth.[52] Depth, feeling, and the body go together in an adult self, making real community possible.

4. *The adult self has clear boundaries.* With clear boundaries, "nothing that belongs inside must be left outside, nothing that must be outside can be tolerated inside."[53] Clear boundaries make for the delineation, coherence, and wholeness of the adult self. "There is," says Jung, "no personality without definiteness, wholeness, and ripeness."[54] With clear boundaries, the adult self, a body-self with feeling and depth, has its own dimension and place in its mutuality with what is other. It is an integral self, and it knows who it is and who it is not. It knows where its own body-self ends, so to speak, and where other body-selves begin. The adult self is able to accept itself and the other as, in Mario Jacobi's phrase, "a Thou in his or her own right."[55] In fact, as Margaret Kornfeld emphasizes, *"Relationships are made when the boundaries of selves are respected."*[56]

To speak of clear boundaries is to speak also of the limits of the self. With clear boundaries, there is an owning of the body-self with its needs and its nature, its strengths and vulnerabilities, its possibilities and failures. The limits of the adult self include what Viktor Frankl calls the "tragic triad" of our existence: suffering, guilt, and death.[57] And yet, with an acceptance of the boundaries and limits of the self, there is an accompanying acceptance of the other, both other persons and other realities in the world. In other words, a boundaried and coherent adult self is, paradoxically, a *contextual self* as well; it is a self that attends to other coherent selves and to a coherent understanding of the world, a world with its own boundaries, needs, and limits. In an adult self as an integral self-in-mutuality, clear boundaries and a context of coherent selves go together, making real community possible.

5. *The adult self exists in intimacy.* Intimacy is the feeling and depth of the body-self welcoming the feeling and depth of the other. The boundaries of the adult self, which are clear and definite, are paradoxically quite penetrable at the same time. It is the very penetrability of these boundaries—evidenced in such qualities as openness, availability, self-forgetfulness, understanding, and love—that makes intimacy possible. Erik Erikson understands intimacy as an "ethical strength," as the capacity to commit oneself to "concrete affiliations

and partnerships."[58] For Erikson, this ethical strength is crucial in sexuality. What he calls "true genitality" is possible only because of intimacy.[59]

Intimacy is also revealed in empathy. To be "in the inner world of the other as if it were your own" is an exercise in intimacy.[60] "Without empathy," says Jordan, "there is no intimacy, no real attainment of an appreciation of the paradox of separateness within connection."[61] Real empathy, which for Rogers is connected with love and is inherently therapeutic, is the ability of the adult self to be with another person, not as one needs that person to be but just as that other person actually is. The empathy and love found in intimacy are at the core of the adult self; they are the natural heirs to the fantasy, the relating in transference, and the logic of objective knowing of the adolescing self. In an adult self as an integral self-in-mutuality, empathy, love, sexuality, and intimacy go together, making real community possible.

6. Finally, along with these other characteristics and as a culmination of them, the adult self is its own responsible process. As long as it is still adolescing, that is, as long as it is still-forming and still-dependent, the self is a kind of "locus of actions and reactions" in the situations in which it finds itself. In fact, because of the way our bodies are attended to as we are growing up, we tend to think of ourselves as objects amid other objects in the world.[62] When we reach adulthood, this objectlike sense of self disappears.[63] As an integral self relating in mutuality to what is other, the adult self, as its own body-self in feeling and in depth, is its own center of responding. "To have a sense of responsibility," asserts William Meissner, "is to have a sense of inner reality and identity."[64] As George Kunz puts it, "I am I because I cannot pass off my responsibilities to any other."[65] In adulthood, integrity and the ability to respond go together, the one unfolding and deepening the other. The adult self is its own responsible process of relating, which maintains a continuity with the past, a meaning for the present, and a direction for the future.[66]

"To be responsible," asserts Richard Niebuhr, "is to be a self in the presence of other selves, to whom one is bound and to whom one is able to answer freely."[67] As an integral self-in-mutuality, the adult self is its own boundaried and coherent process of interaction with others and the world, a process with its own focus, its own sense of purpose and commitment. In being able to grow and to move forward in authentic responsiveness, it experiences itself as able to be and as needing to be responsible. "I am," says Emmanuel Levinas, "he who finds the resources to respond to the call."[68] In fact, my ongoing sense of myself actually depends on my ability to respond to what is other. In adulthood, the responsible self and the call of the other go together. The adult self as an integral self-in-mutuality is a living process, which is its own responsibility, making real community possible.

WAYS OF BEING OF THE ADULT SELF

Flowing from the definition of an adult self as an integral self-in-mutuality and flowing from the six characteristics of this self are two relational ways of being that are the fullness of adult functioning. These two adult ways of being—always woven together in living interaction—are *an actualizing self-in-mutuality* and *a reflecting self-in-mutuality*.[69] These two ways of being are not really possible for us as adolescing selves, because the adolescing self is not yet coherent enough, not yet its own ongoing process. But when we become adult selves, these two ways of being are not only possible but are really quite necessary. The adult self maintains itself and continues to grow as an actualizing and reflecting self-in-mutuality.

1. An adult self: an actualizing self-in-mutuality. An integral adult self is *an actualizing self-in-mutuality*. Flowing back and forth with its reflecting and in tandem with it is the ability of an actualizing self to pursue freely and fully its own path in life.[70] "The course is now set from the bowels of the ship," says William Caspary. "Helmsman, chart, and stars are instrumental to locating and pursuing the course, but the fundamental direction comes from within."[71] The body-self, in its feeling and in its depth, determines for itself how it will move forward. The meanings and values of others no longer dictate its actualization. The adult self is at one with itself. Its purposeful, directed, responsible action comes from within.

An actualizing self-in-mutuality has the ability to live from within its own boundaries, not having its own feeling confused by the feeling of others, not having its own values and actions dictated by the needs of others. But at the same time, and paradoxically, in freely setting its own course in life, the adult self as an actualizing self-in-mutuality also experiences the imperative to weigh the needs and feelings of others. This ability of the actualizing adult self has to do with agency, a sense of mastery, will power, and the ability to act creatively. Yet, often this actualizing is experienced by us as a call, and it seems to be meaningful only within a context of community and "the shared visions of adulthood."[72]

This actualizing turns into caring for others in a responsible way and into various kinds of generativity. The heart of actualizing lies, of course, in making actual life choices. In the morality of making one's own choices, an actualizing adult self keeps itself responsible for how it continues to develop and grow and for the deepening of its relationships with others. Without question, this actualizing is essential to the integrity and the continuing unfolding of the adult self. As an ongoing process, it is a hallmark of adult functioning, and it is what allows personal meaning to emerge and be owned in our ongoing life in community.

2. An adult self: a reflecting self-in-mutuality. An integral adult self is *a reflecting self-in-mutuality.* Flowing back and forth with its actualizing and in tandem with it is the ability of an adult self to capture the meaning and significance of his or her activity. This ability to reflect is the way an adult self finds and continues to hold—in feeling, in depth, with clear boundaries, and in intimacy—who it is with others and the world. Reflecting is a gentle holding and a felt sifting of the body-self's experience so that intention, memory, and meaning can come together and become part of the body-self's ongoing process. Much more than the logic of objective knowing, reflecting is the way we understand ourselves in context with others and the world, and it is the way we gain perspective on our lives.[73]

This reflecting, which at times may be possible only in the presence of an empathic other who genuinely cares for the self, is both a vantage point and a fulcrum to the body-self.[74] It is, paradoxically, the ability "to feel into" and at the same time "to stand outside of" one's own experiencing so that the meaning of our experience becomes clearer as its unfolding story is able to be told. Reflecting is, then, a personal and contextual knowing and valuing that comes from the awareness of one's own feeling, from sensing what is there in the depth, from being with the boundaries of the self, and from being with the feeling and the depth of the other in community.

As we are describing it here, this reflecting is really an understanding of conscience as an ongoing process of the adult self.[75] This personal and contextual knowing and valuing, this conscience, is how the adult self keeps itself responsible for its own continuing development and for the deepening of its relationships with what is other. Without question, reflecting is essential to the integrity and the continuing unfolding of the adult self. As an ongoing process, it is a hallmark of adult functioning, and it is what allows personal meaning to emerge and be owned in our ongoing life in community.

NOTES

1. Abigail J. Stewart and Joseph M. Healy Jr., "Processing Affective Responses to Life Experiences: The Development of the Adult Self," in *Emotion in Adult Development*, ed. Carol Z. Malatesta and Carroll E. Izard (London: Sage, 1984), 282, state that there is a "qualitative difference" to be found in the person when adulthood is reached, and they see the hallmarks of this difference as "the capacity for intimacy, the capacity for commitment and the productive acceptance of personal extinction."

2. See Ernest Becker, *The Denial of Death* (New York: Free Press, 1973).

3. Harold H. Oliver, *Relatedness: Essays in Metaphysics and Theology* (Macon, GA: Mercer University Press, 1984), 162, states, "The notion of selfhood which discloses itself intuitively rather than reflectively is that of the *relational self*. In relational selfhood there is no 'I' separated from a 'Thou'; for the 'experiential other' signals not 'separation,' but 'mutuality.' The very being of the 'I' of 'I-Thou' is a co-being. Accordingly, it is more faithful to experience to say that the 'I' is created by the relation than to say that the 'I' creates the relation through its prior subjectivity. The 'I' emerges with its 'Thou' in the same creative act. Reality thus discloses itself relationally as 'mutuality.'"

4. Emily Souvaine, Lisa L. Lahey, and Robert Kegan, "Life after Formal Operations: Implications for a Psychology of the Self," in *Higher Stages of Human Development: Perspectives on Adult Growth*, ed. Charles N. Alexander and Ellen J. Langer (New York: Oxford, 1990), 234.

5. W. W. Meissner, *Psychoanalysis and Religious Experience* (New Haven, CT: Yale University Press, 1984), 18.

6. Leland Elhard, "Living Faith: Some Contributions of the Concept of Ego-identity to the Understanding of Faith," in *The Dialogue between Theology and Psychology*, ed. Peter Homans (Chicago: University of Chicago Press, 1968), 137.

7. Carl G. Jung, *The Collected Works of C. G. Jung*, vol. 17, *The Development of Personality* (Princeton, NJ: Princeton University Press, 1981), 169.

8. Clifford Geertz, "On the Nature of Anthropological Understanding," *American Scientist* 63 (1975): 49.

9. Erik H. Erikson, *Identity: Youth and Crisis* (New York: Norton, 1968), 87.

10. For some different perspectives on the self-in-relatedness, see John Macmurray, *Persons in Relation* (London: Faber and Faber, 1961). See also Margaret C. Huff, "The Interdependent Self: An Integrated Concept from Feminist Theology and Feminist Psychology," *Philosophy & Theology* 11, no. 2 (Winter 1987): 160–72; Judith V. Jordan, Alexandra G. Kaplan, Jean Baker Miller, Irene P. Stiver, and Janet L. Surrey, eds., *Women's Growth in Connection: Writings from the Stone Center* (New York: Guilford, 1991); Gil G. Noam, "Beyond Freud and Piaget: Biographical Worlds—Interpersonal Self," in *The Moral Domain*, ed. Thomas E. Wren (Cambridge, MA: MIT Press, 1990), 361–99.

11. John McDargh, "God, Mother and Me: An Object Relational Perspective on Religious Material," *Pastoral Psychology* 34, no. 4 (Summer 1986): 255.

12. William Willeford, *Feeling, Imagination, and the Self: Transformations of the Mother-Infant Relationship* (Evanston, IL: Northwestern University Press, 1987), 145.

13. The quote is my adaptation of Kenneth T. Gallagher's "The tie which binds me to others gives me to myself" in *The Philosophy of Gabriel Marcel* (New York: Fordham University Press, 1962), 22. Jerry H. Gill, *Mediated Transcendence: A Postmodern Reflection* (Macon, GA: Mercer University Press, 1989), 152, says, "We begin as beings in relationship, and by means of relationships we come to know ourselves in the world."

14. Paul Ricoeur, *Oneself as Another* (Chicago: University of Chicago Press, 1992), 187.

15. Martin Buber, "Distance and Relation," in *The Knowledge of Man*, trans. Maurice Friedman and Ronald Gregor Smith (New York: Harper & Row, 1965), 71, observes that "the inmost growth of the self is not accomplished, as people like to suppose today, in man's relation to himself, but in the relation between the one and the other, between men, that is, preeminently in the mutuality of the making present—in the making present of another self and in the knowledge that one is made present in his own self by the other—together with the mutuality of acceptance, of affirmation and confirmation."

16. Judith V. Jordan, "The Meaning of Mutuality," in *Women's Growth in Connection*, 82.

17. See Robert Selman, *The Growth of Interpersonal Understanding: Developmental and Clinical Analyses* (New York: Academic Press, 1980).

18. Dawn M. Nothwehr, *Mutuality: A Formal Norm for Christian Ethics* (San Francisco: Catholic Scholars Press, 1998), 5.

19. See John J. Shea, "The Adult Self: Process and Paradox," *Journal of Adult Development* 10, no. 1 (January 2003): 23–30.

20. Shea, "The Adult Self," 23–24.

21. Shea, "The Adult Self," 24. Suzanne R. Kirschner, *The Religious and Romantic Origins of Psychoanalysis: Individuation and Integration in Post-Freudian Theory* (New York: Cambridge University Press, 1996), 63, observes in assessing psychoanalytic theory, "The truly mature self, then, is seen to be characterized by a relative integration of divergent or opposing needs and tendencies, and by a more or less stable resolution of the ongoing tension between the self's infinity of wishes and the limitations of reality."

22. Ricoeur, *Oneself as Another*, 319. The problem with the notion of "embodiment" is pointed out by Thomas Ots, "The Silenced Body—The Expressive *Leib*: On the Dialectic of Mind and Life in Chinese Cathartic Healing," in *Embodiment and Experience: The Existential Ground of Culture and Self*, ed. Thomas J. Csordas (New York: Cambridge University Press, 1994), 117: "The term embodiment may perpetuate the clean subject-object dichotomy of mind and body rather than helping to collapse it."

23. Gabriel Marcel, *Metaphysical Journal* (Chicago: Regnery, 1952), 259.

24. Carl R. Rogers, "A Theory of Therapy, Personality, and Interpersonal Relationships, as Developed in the Client-Centered Framework," in *Psychology:*

CHAPTER 6

A Study of a Science, vol. 3, *Formulations of the Person and the Social Content*, ed. Sigmund Koch (New York: McGraw-Hill, 1959), 205–6.

25. In discussing trauma, Donald Kalsched, *The Inner World of Trauma: Archetypal Defenses of the Personal Spirit* (New York: Routledge, 1996), 67, uses the notion of a "mind/body unity."

26. Bruce Wilshire, *Role Playing and Identity: The Limits of Theatre as Metaphor* (Bloomington: Indiana University Press, 1982), 154, says that the body may be "present without being presented." In an adult body-self, this happens as appropriate.

27. For an excellent discussion of adult commitment, see Richard T. Knowles, *Human Development and Human Possibility: Erikson in the Light of Heidegger* (Lanham, MD: University Press of America, 1986), 129–41.

28. Jerry H. Gill, *On Knowing God* (Philadelphia: Westminster Press, 1981), 70.

29. See Gabriel Marcel, *The Mystery of Being*, 2 vols. (Chicago: Regnery, 1960); see also his *Homo Viator: Introduction to a Metaphysic of Hope* (New York: Harper & Row, 1962).

30. Drew Leder, *The Absent Body* (Chicago: University of Chicago Press, 1990), 128.

31. Kathleen R. Fischer, *Reclaiming the Connection: A Contemporary Spirituality* (Kansas City, MO: Sheed & Ward, 1990), 31.

32. Michael Hardiman, *Ordinary Heroes: A Future for Men* (Dublin: Newleaf, 2000), 37.

33. Wilson Van Dusen, *The Natural Depth in Man* (New York: Harper & Row, 1972), 62.

34. James Nelson, *Between Two Gardens: Reflections on Sexuality and Religious Experience* (New York: Pilgrim, 1983), 10.

35. Marcel, *Metaphysical Journal*, 259–60.

36. David M. Levin, "Eros and Psyche: A Reading of Neumann and Merleau-Ponty," in *Pathways into the Jungian World: Phenomenology and Analytical Psychology*, ed. Roger Brooke (New York: Routledge, 2000), 172.

37. Edward S. Casey, *Spirit and Soul: Essays in Philosophical Psychology* (Dallas, TX: Spring, 1991), xiii.

38. John Heron, *Feeling and Personhood: Psychology in Another Key* (London: Sage, 1992), 93.

39. Carl R. Rogers, "A Process Conception of Psychotherapy," in *On Becoming a Person* (Boston: Houghton Mifflin, 1961), 145–55.

40. Rogers, "A Theory of Therapy," 198; Eugene T. Gendlin, "Experiencing: A Variable in the Process of Therapeutic Change," *The American Journal of Psychotherapy* 15, no. 2 (April 1961): 237.

41. Eugene T. Gendlin, "A Theory of Personality Change," in *New Directions in Client-Centered Therapy*, ed. J. T. Hart and T. M. Tomlinson (Boston: Houghton Mifflin, 1970), 140.

42. Elhard, "Living Faith," 137.

43. Charles Taylor, *Sources of the Self: The Making of the Modern Identity* (Cambridge, MA: Harvard University Press, 1989), 111.

44. Augusto Blasi, "Identity and the Development of the Self," in *Self, Ego, and Identity: Integrative Approaches*, ed. Daniel K. Lapsley and F. Clark Power (New York: Springer-Verlag, 1988), 227.

45. Meissner, *Psychoanalysis and Religious Experience*, 229.

46. Ira Progoff, *Depth Psychology and Modern Man* (New York: McGraw-Hill, 1973), 29.

47. See, for example, Thomas Moore, *Care of the Soul: A Guide for Cultivating Depth and Sacredness in Everyday Life* (New York: HarperCollins, 1992).

48. See, for example, James Hillman, *The Thought of the Heart* (Dallas, TX: Spring, 1984).

49. See, for example, Max Scheler, *Man's Place in Nature* (New York: Noonday, 1962). Writing on the effects of trauma, Kalsched, *The Inner World of Trauma*, 67, observes, "When mind and body split, the animating principle of psychological life, or what we could call spirit, leaves."

50. See Max van Manen and Bas Levering, *Childhood's Secrets: Intimacy, Privacy, and the Self Reconsidered* (New York: Teachers College Press, 1996), 100; see also William James, *The Varieties of Religious Experience* (Cambridge, MA: Harvard University Press, 1985), 402.

51. Carl G. Jung, *The Collected Works of C. G. Jung*, vol. 9, pt. 1, *Archetypes and the Collective Unconscious* (Princeton, NJ: Princeton University Press, 1968), 22.

52. For a good understanding of depth in the context of interpersonal development, see Selman, *The Growth of Interpersonal Understanding*. See also Progoff, *Depth Psychology and Modern Man*.

53. Erik H. Erikson, *Insight and Responsibility* (New York: Norton, 1964), 92.

54. Jung, *The Development of Personality*, 171.

55. Mario Jacobi, *The Analytic Encounter: Transference and Human Relationship* (Toronto: Inner City Books, 1984), 64.

56. Margaret Kornfeld, *Cultivating Wholeness: A Guide to Care and Counseling in Faith Communities* (New York: Continuum, 1998), 292.

57. See Viktor E. Frankl, *The Doctor and the Soul* (New York: Knopf, 1966).

58. Erik H. Erikson, *Childhood and Society*, 2nd ed. (New York: Norton, 1963), 263.

59. Erikson, *Childhood and Society*, 264.

60. Rogers, "A Theory of Therapy," 210.

61. Judith V. Jordan, "Empathy and Self Boundaries," in *Women's Growth in Connection*, 69.

62. See, for example, Jean Piaget, *Six Psychological Studies*, trans. Anita Tenzer (New York: Vintage, 1968), 13.

63. Thomas J. Csordas, "Embodiment as a Paradigm for Anthropology," *Ethos* 18, no. 1 (1990): 36, observes that it is not true "that the fully developed adult moving about in the world treats his or her body as an object."

64. Meissner, *Psychoanalysis and Religious Experience*, 237.

65. George Kunz, *The Paradox of Power and Weakness: Levinas and an Alternative Paradigm for Psychology* (Albany: State University of New York Press, 1998), 33.

66. James E. Marcia, "Common Processes Underlying Ego Identity, Cognitive/Moral Development, and Individuation," in *Self, Ego, and Identity: Integrative Approaches*, ed. Daniel K. Lapsley and F. Clark Power (New York: Springer-Verlag, 1988), 217.

67. H. Richard Niebuhr, "The Responsibility of the Church for Society," in *The Gospel, the Church, and the World*, ed. Kenneth Scott Latourette (New York: Harper & Brothers, 1946), 114.

68. Quoted in Kunz, *The Paradox of Power and Weakness*, 199.

69. Stewart and Healy, "Processing Affective Responses to Life Experiences," 284, characterize the adult self similarly as "the proactive, processing self."

70. Marcia Cavell, "Erik Erikson and the Temporal Mind," in *Ideas and Identities: The Life and Work of Erik Erikson*, ed. Robert S. Wallerstein and Leo Goldberger (Madison, CT: International Universities Press, 1998), 42, captures the sense of self-actualization when she speaks about "the identity of integrated agency."

71. William R. Caspary, "The Concept of a Core-Self," in *The Book of the Self: Person, Pretext, and Process*, ed. Polly Young-Eisendrath and James A. Hall (New York: New York University Press, 1987), 368.

72. Erik H. Erikson, *Toys and Reasons: Stages in the Ritualization of Experience* (New York: Norton, 1977), 45.

73. There are two procedures that may be particularly helpful with accessing our feeling and depth in self-reflection. One is the process of focusing described by Eugene T. Gendlin, *Focusing* (New York: Bantam, 1981). The other is the process of psyche-evoking described by Ira Progoff, *At a Journal Workshop* (Los Angeles: Tarcher, 1992).

74. See Andras Angyal, "The Convergence of Psychotherapy and Religion," *Journal of Pastoral Care* 5, no. 4 (1951): 12.

75. As Jane Loevinger, with the assistance of Augusto Blasi, *Ego Development: Conceptions and Theories* (San Francisco: Jossey-Bass, 1976), 397, observes, "Conscience is above all a reflexive concept."

7

UNFETTERED IMAGING AND RELIGIOUS EXPERIENCING

THE PROCESS OF UNFETTERED IMAGING

The being of the adult self, all of its characteristics, and its full functioning in actualizing and reflecting are possible because the adult self is able to image reality in a way that is whole, complete, and without constraint. While the imaging of reality that lies in the still-forming and still-dependent adolescing self is a fettered process of imaging, the imaging of reality that resides in the adult self is an unfettered, integral process of imaging. In fact, perhaps the simplest way to understand unfettered imaging is to see it as a transformation of fettered imaging.

Unfettered imaging is a process of imaging reality that is no longer embedded, as is fettered imaging, in elements of fantasy. Unfettered imaging is a process of imaging other selves that is no longer distorted, as is fettered imaging, by relating in transference.[1] Unfettered imaging is a process of imaging the world that is no longer confined, as is fettered imaging, by the logic of objective knowing. Unfettered imaging is our unique process of imaging reality in which we are no longer held bound, as in fettered imaging, by the meanings and values put forth by others. Quite simply, our unfettered imaging, as the notion suggests, is now our own, appropriate, liberated process of imaging.

To say that unfettered imaging is an adult process of imaging is to say, of course, that it is a whole process of imaging that is directly and completely in and of the adult self. Unfettered imaging is an imaging of reality that is fully authored by and fully owned by the adult self as an actualizing and reflecting self-in-mutuality. Because unfettered imaging is an adult imaging of reality, it allows us to experience things as they really are. It allows us to have what Kenneth Bragan describes as "a reality untainted by preconception or by distortion."[2] It allows us to have what Mark Johnson describes as a "coherent and unified experience or understanding."[3] And yet—crucial as it is both for adulthood and for adult religion—unfettered imaging is often completely ignored. A fettered, dichotomized, homogenized, and thoroughly disembodied understanding of how we image reality is so pervasive in the culture that we hardly have any available vocabulary to help us become aware of our unfettered imaging when it is occurring, let alone to be able to describe it.

The problem, especially in the last several centuries, is that almost unquestionably an adult imaging of reality is presumed to be something of "the mind" in separation from the body. If it is an adult imaging of reality, it must be "empirical," and it must be "objective." It may be nearly impossible, therefore, to think that adult imaging is something of the whole body-self. Unquestionably, an adult imaging of reality is presumed to occur through a logic of objective knowing. A mature imaging of reality must be "reasoned" and not contaminated by anything "personal" or "subjective." It may be nearly impossible, therefore, to think that adult imaging is necessarily something of feeling and of depth. The truth is, however, that adult or unfettered imaging does not come from how the mind sees reality; nor does it really depend on the logic of objective knowing.

As we have seen, unfettered imaging is something directly and completely in and of the adult self. It is, therefore, understood best in light of the definition of this self and in light of its six characteristics.[4]

The unfettered imaging of adulthood is of the self as *an integral self-in-mutuality*. That is to say, unfettered imaging is the adult self, as the wholeness of its own self, relating in mutuality to what is other than itself. It is the process of imaging of the formed, interdependent self as it grasps, understands, and relates in mutuality to other persons and to the other meaningful wholes to be found in reality. Although we may rely on a cameralike notion of "the mind" to describe how we "see" what is there in "objective reality," and although "images in the mind" may serve as a partial description of fettered imaging, such a description is completely inadequate as an understanding of adult imaging. The unfettered imaging of adulthood is of the self as an integral self-in-mutuality. It is an ongoing, integral imaging of reality in which the adult self in all its characteristics relates in mutuality to reality as a whole.

1. The unfettered imaging of adulthood is in and of the body-self. Contrary to the ideals of the Platonic and Cartesian traditions in philosophy, unfettered imaging has nothing to do with breaking away from the confines of the body.[5] "We encounter reality," says Jerry Gill, "as holistic, integral beings who interact with the world in and through all the dimensions of bodily existence simultaneously."[6] In adulthood, the body does not fetter imaging. On the contrary, unfettered imaging is possible only through the full appropriation of the body. Unfettered imaging takes place only when the mind is in harmony with the experiencing of the body. It is a knowing of reality possible for us only in the oneness and completeness of the body-self.[7] The unfettered imaging of adulthood is of the body-self. It is never just static mental images. It is never two-dimensional pictures of a world with no depth. The fullness of human imaging demands the integrity of the body-self.

2. The unfettered imaging of adulthood is in feeling. In fact, unfettered imaging is always a felt imaging; it is an imaging that is bodily felt and meaningful at the same time.[8] We conveniently speak of imaging as if it were something in our minds and not connected to our bodies, but unfettered imaging is never just thoughts or pictures in the mind— no matter how clear and distinct they may be. Rather, unfettered imaging is necessarily embodied. Truth is felt; care is felt; justice is felt. Feeling is felt-in-the-whole-body thinking; feeling is felt-in-the-whole-body perceiving; feeling is felt-in-the-whole-body knowing; and feeling is felt-in-the-whole-body meaning. Thought and emotion are one because in the body-self they are experienced as one. The unfettered imaging of adulthood, the fullness of human imaging, is the ongoing feeling of the body-self. It is our presently alive, felt, interactive process of knowing and understanding.

---

3. The unfettered imaging of adulthood is the depth of the body-self.
The thinking of Ira Progoff suggests this most clearly. He says the depth is a "flow of imaging."[9] Progoff is pointing to the fact that this imaging touches and reveals the "more" or the "other" in a way that is integral and directing for the self and yet in a way that cannot be objectively known or controlled by the mind. Although we may speak of our unfettered imaging as if it were images in our minds, unfettered imaging is actually a three-dimensional, holistic process of the body-self. Progoff understands *"wholeness in depth* as the most adequate way to understand the magnitude of human nature."[10] The unfettered imagining of adulthood, the fullness of human imaging, is a "wholeness in depth." It is the sensing and intuiting depth of the body-self.

4. The unfettered imaging of adulthood is within clear boundaries.
It is the boundaries of the coherent, delineated, integral self that allow for an imaging of reality that is equally delineated, equally coherent, and equally in terms of meaningful wholes. Only in a self with clear boundaries is an adult knowing of reality possible. Only in a self with clear boundaries is a "coherent and unified experience or understanding" of reality able to occur.[11] Although we may think of our unfettered imaging as something occurring in our minds, it is only clear boundaries that allow this adult imaging to happen. The unfettered imaging of adulthood, which is the fullness of human imaging, is a process within clear boundaries.

5. The unfettered imaging of adulthood lives in intimacy. Not only is this true because in intimacy the other person can now be appreciated as a "whole subject,"[12] but this is true also because only in a context of love, and intimacy, and empathy do we really seem to experience unfettered imaging. Richard Kearney alludes to this when he points out that "imagination is always a response to the demands of an other existing beyond the self."[13] Unfettered imaging arises for us in a context of intimacy. Although we may become aware of this imaging as if it were something in our minds, only intimacy allows this integral kind of imaging to form. The unfettered imaging of adulthood, which is the fullness of human imaging, is a process that lives in intimacy.

6. The unfettered imaging of adulthood is a responsible process. Our unfettered imaging is the fullness of imaging as its own process, as a process that is its own responsibility. In this last characteristic of unfettered imaging, a characteristic that is the culmination of all the others, unfettered imaging is understood as a responsible process of integrity that lies in the self—and really it is the responsible process that *is* the adult self. That is why unfettered imaging could never be "mental images" or "pictures in the mind." Quite simply, the unfettered imaging of adulthood is the adult self relating to reality as its own responsible process.

RELIGIOUS EXPERIENCING

As important as unfettered imaging is for understanding an appropriation of adult reality, we are interested in this integral form of imaging because of what it makes possible in the imaging of God. If fantasy, relating in transference, and the logic of objective knowing are strands of fettered imaging that let us find a Superego God, how can we describe the integral imaging that helps us find a Living God? How can we name the unfettered imaging of God of which the adult self is capable? The answer lies, I believe, in a notion of "religious experiencing." As an integral imaging of God, religious experiencing can be understood as the grasp of God of the adult self. It is not surprising, therefore, that religious experiencing, which comes directly and completely from the adult self, gets its clearest description in light of the definition of this self along with its six characteristics.[14]

Religious experiencing is essentially in and of *an integral self-in-mutuality*. Integrity is the basis on which we are our whole, coherent selves, not just with what is other, but also with our God. "Faith," as Leland Elhard puts it, "is really saying 'I' in the presence of God, finding all the experiences, part-identifications, and images of the past given unity, continuity, and mastery" in the living interaction with God.[15] It is because of the integrity of the self-in-mutuality that mutuality with God, that is, a real dialogue, a give and take, can occur.[16] Again speaking of faith, Elhard captures the integral sense of this mutuality when he says:

Faith is the self constituted by God's relating to it. In this normative definition faith and identity coincide. Here, the relationship of God with a man [*sic*] uninterruptedly forms man's relationship with himself. God's recognition becomes the self-realization and self-recognition of the self. I mean most to myself when I mean most to God when God means most to me.[17]

1. Religious experiencing presupposes a body-self. Religious experiencing is always an incarnation, always something that is in and of the wholeness of the body-self. Religious experiencing is much more than assent in the mind to a set of beliefs. An adult relationship with God is much more than formal adherence to a given denomination or religious tradition. The experience of God in adult religion is not just in our concepts and creeds; rather, the concepts and creeds have personal meaning because they resonate or ring true with our actual bodily knowing. As Christopher Bryant points out, "the experience of God is no mere intellectual knowledge. It is heart-knowledge, in which emotion and instinct, intuition and the irrational, body as well as soul must participate."[18]

2. Religious experiencing is founded in feeling. "I do believe," says William James, "that feeling is the deeper source of religion, and that philosophic and theological formulas are secondary products like translations of a text into another tongue."[19] Paul Clifford calls feeling "a diffused recognition of transcendent mystery—the sense of the numinous, as Otto called it—which both precedes and underlies all attempts at theological clarification and discourse."[20] Our feeling is the locus or "place" to find, to be with, and to know God, a place which is in and of the wholeness of the body-self, a place of "felt meaning" where what we know and what we feel live together in integrity.

3. Religious experiencing has a sense of depth. One aspect of this felt depth is captured well by William James, who, in reference to the logic of objective knowing, observes:

> It is as if there were in the human consciousness a *sense of reality, a feeling of objective presence, a perception* of what we may call "something there," more deep and more general than any of the special and particular "senses" by which the current psychology supposes existent realities to be originally revealed.[21]

Bryant notes that the experience of God is "a mystery that we can dimly sense but cannot grasp."[22] In the depth, the self and the presence of God are revealed together. "As we find our way of living in depth in relationship with people, events, and things around us, we may begin to hear," says Vincent Bilotta, "the nearness of the presence of God."[23] This is a central theme in Carl Jung's whole understanding of the process of individuation.[24] We experience the reality of God in images and intimations that come from the depth and that are known only in the language of metaphor and symbol. In religious experiencing, the soul, the heart, and the spirit echo the depth and the mystery of God. In the words of the mystic Angelus Silesius:

> The abyss that is my soul invokes unceasingly
> The abyss that is my God. Which may the deeper be? (1:68)[25]

4. Religious experiencing has clear boundaries as well. In an adult relationship with God, our boundaries as adult selves are what allow us to understand the boundaries of God. The meaningful "wholeness" of the adult self is what allows for an understanding of the meaningful "wholeness" of God. In other words, as reasonably coherent adult selves, we do not need to project a lot that is "unfulfilled, unlived, and unexpressed" onto the reality of God.[26] An adult self that knows itself and can respect its own boundaries and limitations is able to know and respect the boundaries and limitations of God—in honesty, humility, and without a great need for control. In religious experiencing, the paradox that "one is fully God's self and fully one's self at the same time" is only possible because of the integrity of clear boundaries.[27]

5. Religious experiencing exists in intimacy. In religious experiencing, the self and the reality of God are now together in an intimacy in which sexual images are often most appropriate. The adult self is known in or with God, not that this self is perfect in the relationship, but that it fully lives the relationship. As Ann Ulanov remarks:

> What God asks is a living relationship, an "I am," an "I am who is," an "I am with you." What God wants is an answering "I am" too, one that says, "Here I am too. I am with you."[28]

Saint Augustine, a man who by his own account was recovering from sexual addiction, also found a sense of intimacy with God. In his *Confessions*, his prayer to God is, "You were closer to me than I was to myself."[29] Saint Thérèse of Lisieux, whose life was also not without difficulties, writes of the love of her intimate yet absent God: "In my childhood, your love was there waiting for me; as I grew up, it grew with me; and now it is like a great chasm whose depths are past sounding."[30]

6. Religious experiencing is its own responsible process. Now the self and God are together as an ongoing process of experiencing. Religious *experience* is now an integral process, is now religious *experiencing*, as our meaning and the meaning of God unfold together.[31] Religious experiencing is its own unique, responsible process in which we move in God even as we find God moving in us. In this process, the self is growing and moving forward as an integral self-in-mutuality with God. Religious experiencing is both process and paradox. To be responsible to ourselves is to be responsible to God, and to be responsible to God is to be responsible to ourselves.

In addition to these six characteristics, religious experiencing also has two ways of being, two ongoing ways the self and God exist together.

1. Religious experiencing is an actualizing self-in-mutuality. In this actualizing lies all the concrete choices and actions that further both others and ourselves even as they further our relationship with God.[32] Actualizing is in and of the body-self in its feeling and in its depth in relation to God, and it is a way of enhancing the boundaries of the self, the intimacy of relating, and the sense of our being a responsible process with God. It is really a way for the adult self to be in God as a *creative process* of ongoing religious experiencing. At times, this actualizing may come from responding to the will of God. At times, it may come through the different kinds of work, service, or ministry we engage in. At times, it may come through actions that build up the community. At times, it may come through our acts of love, compassion, caring, and the pursuit of justice. Whatever its different modes may be, our actualizing is essential to having and holding religious experiencing. Actualizing—or what is often called "action" in the tradition—is the way we and God actually live together in mutual integrity.

2. Religious experiencing is a reflecting self-in-mutuality. This reflecting is an attending to and a sorting out of how the adult self lives
in the presence of God.[33] Reflecting is paying attention to the body-
self, to feeling, and to the depth in relation to God, and it is the way we
hold the boundaries of the self, our intimacy of relating, and our sense
of being a responsible process with God. This reflecting is really a way
for us to be with God as a *creative process* of ongoing religious experiencing. At times, this reflecting in God may come through the scrip-
tures or through other reading. At times, it may come in prayer, in worship, or in other liturgical services. At times, it may come from
experiencing the love and kindness of others. At times, it may come
through a process of discernment or through meditation and contemplation. At times, it may come through being in nature. Whatever its
different modes may be, reflecting is essential to having and holding
religious experiencing. Reflecting—or what is often called "contemplation" in the tradition—is the way we and God actually live together
in mutual integrity.

Finally, before we look at the characteristics of the Living God that
flow from religious experiencing, it should be pointed out that what
we are describing here as a notion of religious experiencing is something that is often referred to as mystical knowing. When William
James observes in *The Varieties of Religious Experience* that "personal
religious experience has its roots and centre in mystical states of consciousness,"[34] he is saying that religious experience is essentially mystical experience. Interestingly enough, although not using the language of adulthood, James also finds that mystical experience is
appropriate in the self that is, in his words, "no longer divided."[35]
Mystical experience is appropriate in a self that no longer suffers from
the dichotomies of mind-body and subject-object. Quite simply—and
following James's lead—we are able to say that an *adult experiencing
of God is mystical experiencing.*

In other words, when the fettered imaging that lets us find a Superego God is able to be outgrown, there is nothing left to separate the self
from the Living God.[36] The developmental realities of fantasy, relating
in transference, and the logic of objective knowing render mediate and
secondhand a reality that can be experienced and known immediately

and directly. These three strands of fettered imaging keep religious experience from being what it is inherently meant to be, an immediate and first-hand knowing of God in empathy and love with us and an immediate and first-hand knowing of ourselves in empathy and love with God—and this is mystical knowing. In an adult self as an integral self-in-mutuality, the process of unfettered imaging, religious experiencing, and mystical knowing all go together.[37]

NOTES

1. H. C. Rümke, *The Psychology of Unbelief*, trans. M. H. C. Willems (New York: Sheed & Ward, 1962), 50, could be referring to unfettered imaging when he observes, "Relationship with the worldly father must be clear before the God-image can be pure."

2. Kenneth Bragan, *Self and Spirit in the Therapeutic Relationship* (London: Routledge, 1996), 81.

3. Mark Johnson, *The Body in the Mind: The Bodily Basis of Meaning, Imagination, and Reason* (Chicago: University of Chicago Press, 1987), 157.

4. As Susan Hekman, *Moral Voices, Moral Selves: Carol Gilligan and Feminist Moral Theory* (University Park: Pennsylvania State University Press, 1995), 69, points out, "what we know and who we are cannot be neatly separated."

5. It could be, in part, that the need to break away from the confines of the body is actually a need to be free of fettered imaging with its fantasy, transference, and logic of objective knowing.

6. Jerry H. Gill, *Mediated Transcendence: A Postmodern Reflection* (Macon, GA: Mercer University Press, 1989), 67.

7. The body-self lives in paradox. As Drew Leder, *The Absent Body* (Chicago: University of Chicago Press, 1990), 103, suggests, "The body is never a simple presence, but that which is away from itself, a being of difference and absence."

8. See Eugene T. Gendlin, *Focusing-Oriented Psychotherapy: A Manual of the Experiential Method* (New York: Guilford, 1996). The notions of "feeling" and "bodily felt" are central in the unique way of paying attention to the body involved in focusing.

9. See Ira Progoff, *The Symbolic and the Real* (New York: McGraw-Hill, 1963).

10. Progoff, *Depth Psychology and Modern Man*, 13.

11. Johnson, *The Body in the Mind*, 157.

12. Mario Jacobi, *The Analytic Encounter: Transference and Human Relationship* (Toronto: Inner City Books, 1984), 64.

13. Richard Kearney, *The Wake of the Imagination: Toward a Postmodern Culture* (Minneapolis: University of Minnesota Press, 1988), 390.

14. For a process understanding of religious experiencing, see John J. Shea, *Religious Experiencing: William James and Eugene Gendlin* (Lanham, MD: University Press of America, 1987).

15. Leland Elhard, "Living Faith: Some Contributions of the Concept of Ego-identity to the Understanding of Faith," in *The Dialogue Between Theology and Psychology*, ed. Peter Homans, 135–61 (Chicago: University of Chicago Press, 1968), 155.

16. If there were an adult practical theology of the *imago Dei*, that is, if there were an adult practical theology elaborated on the basis of religious experiencing, then God would emerge in this theology as an Integral Self-in-Mutuality.

17. Elhard, "Living Faith," 151.

18. Christopher Bryant, *Jung and the Christian Way* (Minneapolis, MN: Seabury Press, 1984), 52.

19. William James, *The Varieties of Religious Experience* (Cambridge, MA: Harvard University Press, 1985), 341.

20. Paul R. Clifford, "The Place of Feeling in Religious Awareness," in *New Theology, No. 7: The Recovery of Transcendence*, ed. Martin E. Marty and Dean G. Peerman (New York: Macmillan, 1970), 50.

21. James, *Varieties of Religious Experience*, 55.

22. Christopher Bryant, *Depth Psychology and Religious Belief* (London: Darton, Longman & Todd, 1987), 69.

23. Vincent M. Bilotta III, "Originality, Ordinary Intimacy and the Spiritual Life: Welcome! Make Yourself At-home," *Studies in Formative Spirituality* 1, no. 1 (February 1980): 90.

24. See Carl G. Jung, *The Collected Works of C. G. Jung*, vol. 9, pt. 1, *Archetypes and the Collective Unconscious* (Princeton, NJ: Princeton University Press, 1968); see also Jung, *The Collected Works of C. G. Jung*, vol. 9, pt. 2, *Aion: Researches into the Phenomenology of the Self* (Princeton, NJ: Princeton University Press, 1979).

25. Angelus Silesius, *The Cherubinic Wanderer*, trans. Maria Shrady (New York: Paulist Press, 1986), 42.

26. Peter Homans, "Toward a Psychology of Religion: By Way of Freud and Tillich," in *The Dialogue between Theology and Psychology*, ed. Peter Homans (Chicago: University of Chicago Press, 1968), 65.

27. Elhard, "Living Faith," 153.

28. Ann B. Ulanov, *The Wisdom of the Psyche* (Cambridge, MA: Cowley, 1988), 5.

29. In Latin, *Tu autem eras interior intimo meo* (Aurelius Augustinus, *Confessiones*, III, 6, 11).

30. Thérèse of Lisieux, *Autobiography of a Saint*, trans. Ronald Knox (London: Harvill, 1958), 308.

31. See Shea, *Religious Experiencing*.

32. What is described here is referred to in some spiritual traditions as "action."

33. What is described here is referred to in some spiritual traditions as "contemplation."

34. James, *Varieties of Religious Experience*, 301.

35. See especially James, "Lecture VIII: The Divided Self and the Process of Its Unification," in *Varieties of Religious Experience*, 139–56.

36. For an interesting discussion of how mystical experience surfaces in later adulthood, see Jeff Levin, "'Bumping the Top': Is Mysticism the Future of Religious Gerontology?" in *Aging, Spirituality, and Religion: A Handbook*, vol. 2, ed. Melvin A. Kimble and Susan H. McFadden (Minneapolis, MN: Fortress, 2003), 402–11.

37. For Freud and for many others, psychology and religion part company over the issue of adulthood. The wonderful and amazing irony is that *it is only in adulthood that psychology and religion can really come together.*

8

CHARACTERISTICS OF THE LIVING GOD

In religious experiencing, rooted as it is in unfettered imaging, an adult self is able to realize a Living God. From one perspective, as this Living God actually comes to be imaged in a person's life, it can take any number of configurations. This God comes in any number of different experiences and is not the same for everyone. This, of course, should not be surprising. The Living God is experienced immediately and directly by the adult self, and each adult self has his or her unique, self-authored, self-owned way of religious experiencing. At the same time, however, there are some definite characteristics of the Living God that can be accurately described, and this, I believe, is somewhat surprising. Five such characteristics are offered here, each one reflecting some aspect of how the adult self in integral imaging finds the Living God:

1. The Living God is a God as Thou.
2. The Living God is a God of Love.
3. The Living God is a God of Mystery.
4. The Living God is a God of Freedom.
5. The Living God is a God of Community.

In each of these five characteristics, there is a common dynamic at play between the adult self and the Living God. To begin with, each of these five characteristics is a definite statement that captures the *experiencing* of who this God actually *is* for someone at the adult level. Along with this definite statement about who this God is, often there is an *experience of salvation* that is found in the feeling and depth of the self. Moreover, this experience of salvation is had *without condition*. The adult self can be just as it is in the presence of the Living God.

As the relationship between the adult self and the Living God unfolds, it is revealed as a *living paradox*. The "more" of the self is somehow also in the "more" of God. Through ongoing actualizing and reflecting, the adult self finds a *mutual indwelling* with the Living God. In this mutual indwelling, there is a kind of *synergy*, or shared interactive energy, an empowerment in God that makes the adult self more its own integral process even as it moves the self deeper into the reality of the Living God.

Finally, all of the characteristics of the Living God are *transformations* of the characteristics of the Superego God. These transformations are in effect a realization of fullness, a shift from the contradiction of the Superego God to the paradox of the Living God. What was formerly a promise of security is transformed into an experience of salvation. What were formerly experiences of ambivalence and conflict on the superego level are transformed now into a kind of *hopeful expectation* on the adult level. What was formerly a modus vivendi is transformed now into a *living relationship of mutuality* between the adult self and the Living God, and the *response* of the adult self in this living relationship is basically one of trust and love.

1. The Living God is a God as Thou. An adult self in unfettered imaging often relies on the notion of "Thou" or on some other notion of "Spiritual Reality" to say how he or she is actually experiencing the reality of God.[1] This God as Thou is an encompassing, personal, and unique reality, which the adult self is able to encounter freely, uniquely, intimately, and in integrity. In this encounter, there is "real meeting and betweenness."[2] As Peter Homans observes, "in the I-Thou relation meeting replaces knowledge, the existential replaces the merely epistemological, and, therefore, subject and object coexist in unanalyzable integrity and wholeness."[3] As Charles Kao says, "I and Thou are integrated and yet differentiated."[4] Essentially, the experiencing of this God as Thou, which resonates in the feeling and depth of the body-self, is an experience of salvation. That is to say, it is an experience of healing or of the adult self being brought into some greater wholeness. This salvation is experienced as being without condition. In the presence of a God as Thou or Spiritual Reality, the adult self can be just as it is.

In the relationship of the adult self with God as Thou, what seems to arise is a living paradox. At one and the same time, this God is other-than-the-self and not other-than-the-self. Objective distance collapses into a personal closeness that categories of time and place are not really able to capture. This God is now a reality beyond object or person, and yet this God is a mystical reality that seems to invite us into relationship. In various kinds of actualizing and reflecting, we find ourselves in a mutual indwelling with a God as Thou or a Spiritual Reality, and in this mutual indwelling, we experience a synergy or shared interactive energy, an empowerment in God that makes us more our own integral process. This empowerment expands us and moves us more deeply into the reality of the God as Thou or moves us more deeply into the Spiritual Reality.

The God as Thou or the Spiritual Reality is a transformation of the Supreme Being of the adolescing self. In this transformation, the contradiction of the distant, over-against God is somehow changed into the paradox of a God who is experienced as a God of Presence and a God of Absence. In this transformation, the "external" God does not simply become "internal," but rather the subject-object dichotomy is itself transformed so that now the self and God are now felt as completely distinct, suggesting absence, and also as inseparably together, suggesting presence. In this transformation, the ambivalent feeling and the conflict associated with the Supreme Being are also transformed. Now what we seem to feel is a kind of hopeful anticipation as the promise of security is transformed into the experience of salvation. The God as Thou or the Spiritual Reality unites with the adult self in a living relationship of mutuality, and in this living relationship, our response is often one of greater fidelity and love.

2. *The Living God is a God of Love.* An adult self with unfettered imaging often relies on the notion of "Love" to say how he or she is actually experiencing the reality of God. This God of Love is an encompassing,

personal, and unique reality, which the adult self is able to relate to freely, uniquely, intimately, and in integrity. Often the experiencing of this God of Love is very profound, and the adult self finds that it needs to respond in kind. The experiencing of this God of Love, which resonates in the feeling and depth of the body-self, is an experience of salvation. That is to say, it is an experience of healing or of the adult self being brought into some greater wholeness. Salvation is experienced as being without condition. In the presence of the God of Love, the adult self can be just as it is.

As our relationship with the God of Love unfolds, what seems to arise is a living paradox. The God of Love is in the law and beyond the law at the same time. Morality is now understood as a relationship with the God of Love. Also, there is with the God of Love the "acceptance of the unacceptable";[5] this God is a God of Unconditional Acceptance. The God of Love is, as well, a God of Good and Evil, but now somehow evil is, in William James's phrase, "swallowed up in supernatural good."[6] There are various evils in us, and there are various evils in the world, but these evils are not experienced as the last word. The God of Love is somehow beyond right and wrong and beyond good and evil. In various kinds of actualizing and reflecting, we find ourselves in mutual indwelling with the God of Love, and in this mutual indwelling, we experience a synergy, or shared interactive energy, an empowerment in God that makes us even more our own integral process. This empowerment expands us and moves us deeper into the reality of the God of Love.

The God of Love is a transformation of the God of Law. This transformation does not necessarily mean that the laws and the commandments of the Superego God are not binding. Rather, what seems to happen is that these laws and commands are themselves transformed by the paradox of a God of Conscience and a God of Personal Responsibility. The ambivalent feeling and the conflict are transformed as well, and we seem to feel a kind of hopeful anticipation as the promise of security is transformed into the experience of salvation. The God of Love unites with the adult self in a living relationship of mutuality, and in this living relationship, our response is usually one of more love and care for others and an increase in respect for the demands of justice.

3. The Living God is a God of Mystery. An adult self with unfettered imaging often relies on the notion of "Mystery" to say how he or she is actually experiencing the reality of God. The God of Mystery is an encompassing, personal, and unique reality that the adult self is able to encounter freely, uniquely, intimately, and in integrity. Often the experiencing of this God of Mystery is utterly profound, and the adult self finds itself responding to it in wonder and awe. The experiencing of this God of Mystery, which resonates in the feeling and depth of the body-self, is an experience of salvation. That is to say, it is an experience of healing or of the adult self being brought into some greater wholeness. Salvation is experienced as being without condition. In the presence of the God of Mystery, the adult self can be just as it is.

As our relationship with a God of Mystery unfolds, what seems to arise is a living paradox. The God who must be objectively known cannot be known at all, and the God who cannot be known is somehow known anyway. The God of Mystery points to "a reality which is experienced but whose inexhaustible depths and breadth our powers can never encompass."[7] Understanding that there is no adequate understanding of God is somehow a more adequate understanding of God. Therefore, "whatever we say of God is uttered against the silence of a deeper and more fundamental nescience."[8] The right beliefs are still important to us, and yet they may not seem to be important at all. In various kinds of actualizing and reflecting, we find ourselves in mutual indwelling with the God of Mystery, and in this mutual indwelling, we experience a synergy, or shared interactive energy, an empowerment in God that makes us even more our own integral process. This empowerment expands us and moves us deeper into the reality of the God of Mystery.

The God of Mystery is a transformation of the God of Belief. It is not that the concepts and propositions about the Supreme Being are not true, but they are now transformed into a God of Relationship. The logic of objective knowing is transformed into a personal, relational, mystical knowing. Conceptual thinking is transformed into dialectical, hermeneutical, and unitive thinking.[9] The ambivalent feeling and the conflict are transformed as well. Now we seem to feel a kind of hopeful anticipation as the promise of security is transformed into the experience of salvation. The God of Mystery unites with the adult self in a living relationship of mutuality, and in this living relationship, our response is often one of profound wonder, peace, and joy.

4. The Living God is a God of Freedom. An adult self with unfettered imaging often seems to rely on the notion of "Freedom" to say how he or she is actually experiencing the reality of this God. This God of Freedom is an encompassing, personal, and unique reality, which the adult self is able to encounter freely, uniquely, intimately, and in integrity. Often the experiencing of the God of Freedom is quite disarming, and the adult self finds that it wants to respond with a strange kind of self-surrender or openness. The experiencing of the God of Freedom, which resonates in the feeling and depth of the body-self, is an experience of salvation. That is to say, it is an experience of healing or of the adult self being brought into some greater wholeness. Salvation is experienced as being without condition. In the presence of the God of Freedom, the adult self can be just as it is.

As our relationship with the God of Freedom unfolds, what seems to arise is a living paradox. We surrender to a God who invites us to be free, and often our full realization of the freedom comes from the surrendering. Freedom and control are now somehow together for us. In surrendering to God, we find freedom, but in this surrendering, nothing important is really lost. In various kinds of actualizing and reflecting, we find ourselves in mutual indwelling with the God of Freedom, and in this mutual indwelling, we experience a synergy, or shared interactive energy, an empowerment in God that makes us even more our own integral process. This empowerment expands us and moves us deeper into the reality of the God of Freedom.

The God of Freedom is a transformation of the God of Dependency and Control. The contradiction of the God of Dependency and Control is now transformed into the paradox of a God of Mutuality, and with this God there is no need either to control or to be controlled. Our struggle for freedom from God is transformed into a welcome freedom in God. The ambivalent feeling and the conflict are transformed as well. Now we seem to feel a kind of hopeful anticipation as the promise of security is transformed into the experience of salvation. The God of Freedom unites with us in a living relationship of mutuality, and in this living relationship, our response is often one of even greater responsibility and freedom.

5. *The Living God is a God of Community.* An adult self with un-fettered imaging often seems to rely on the notion of "Community" to say how he or she is actually experiencing the reality of God. The God of Community is an encompassing, personal, and unique reality, which the adult self is able to encounter freely, uniquely, intimately, and in integrity. Often the experiencing of the God of Community is deeply authenticating and enlivening, and the adult self finds that it is so much at home that it wants to give back to the God of Community what it receives from it. The experiencing of the God of Community, which resonates in the feeling and depth of the body-self, is an experience of salvation. That is to say, it is an experience of healing or of the adult self being brought into some greater wholeness. Salvation is experienced as being without condition. In the presence of the God of Community, the adult self can be just as it is.

In our relationship with the God of Community, what seems to arise is a living paradox. We have our personal experience of God by sharing this experiencing with others, and in fact, we can only have this experiencing of God for ourselves when we are able to find this experiencing in others. In various kinds of actualizing and reflecting, we find ourselves in mutual indwelling with the God of Community, and in this mutual indwelling there is a synergy, or shared interactive energy, an empowerment in God that makes us even more our own integral process. This empowerment expands us and moves us deeper into the reality of the God of Community.

The God of Community is a transformation of the God of the Group. In this transformation, the contradiction of the controlling, dichotomizing, and homogenizing God of the Group is transformed into the paradox of a God of Communion, a God who invites a diversity of adult selves to come together in some greater unity. The ambivalent feeling and the conflict are transformed as well. Now we seem to feel a kind of hopeful anticipation as the promise of security is transformed into the experience of salvation. The God of Community unites with the adult self in a living relationship of mutuality, and in this living relationship our response is often an increase of compassion along with an increase of mutual love, mutual caring, mutual respect, and mutual concern—all reaching across boundaries.

NOTES

1. For some persons, it seems, to name God in personal terms is too anthropomorphic, not because God is impersonal but because God is not a person.

2. Peter Homans, "Transference and Transcendence: Freud and Tillich on the Nature of Personal Relatedness," *Journal of Religion* 46, no. 1, pt. 2 (1966): 156.

3. Homans, "Transference and Transcendence," 156.

4. Charles C. L. Kao, "Maturity, Spirituality, and Theological Reconstruction," in *Maturity and the Quest for Spiritual Meaning*, ed. Charles C. L. Kao (Lanham, MD: University Press of America, 1988), 45.

5. Carl R. Rogers, "Paul Tillich and Carl Rogers: A Dialogue," *Pastoral Psychology* 19 (February 1968): 59.

6. William James, *The Varieties of Religious Experience* (Cambridge, MA: Harvard University Press, 1985), 131.

7. J. Norman King, *Experiencing God All Ways and Every Day* (Minneapolis, MN: Winston, 1982), 29.

8. Nicholas Lash, "Incarnate and Determinate Freedom," in *On Freedom*, ed. Leroy S. Rouner (Notre Dame, IN: University of Notre Dame Press, 1989), 23.

9. See, for example, Michael Basseches, *Dialectical Thinking and Adult Development* (Norwood, NJ: Ablex, 1984); see also Herb Koplowitz, "Unitary Thought: A Projection beyond Piaget's Formal Operations Stage" (manuscript, Addiction Research Foundation, Simcoe, Ontario, May 1978).

ADULT RELIGION AND INTEGRAL SPIRITUALITY

As we have seen, religion is about "the self and God together." Religion is relational, and it is developmental. Adult religion, made possible as it is by the unfettered imaging of religious experiencing, is about the adult self and the Living God together. At this point, we are able to describe the nature of adult religion in more detail by looking directly at the interaction of the self and God in its mature form. How does the adult self hear and communicate with the Living God?

HEARING THE LIVING GOD

The voice of the Living God that the adult self is able to hear is the voice of God as Thou or the voice of the Spiritual Reality, welcoming the self and inviting relationship. It is the voice of the God of Love, accepting the self without condition and inviting the self to dwell in mutual love. It is the voice of the God of Mystery, calling the self to an understanding of deeper reality and inviting the self to dwell in the mystery. It is the voice of the God of Freedom, supporting the self in the way it needs to grow and inviting the self to dwell in the freedom. And it is the voice of the God of Community, affirming the self in its own unique experience and inviting the self to dwell in community.

This voice of the Living God resonates in the whole body. It is a voice heard in the body-self, a voice heard in feeling and in depth rather than in the mind. Instead of being an external voice of powerful authority, the voice of the Living God is experienced as an inner voice that calls us in a way that does not violate the boundaries of the adult self. This inner voice, even when it is insistent, serves not to diminish or disparage the self but rather to understand the self as it is and to allow the self to respond and move forward. This voice of the Living God is a voice of genuine care for the adult self, and it is a voice of genuine care for others as well. Unlike the voice of the Superego God, which is often authoritarian and "cosmic, vast, and mysterious,"[1] the voice of the Living God is personal, gentle, and full of respect. This voice may be slow to speak, and it may be hard to hear because it resonates in the body-self, and it speaks the more subtle language of feeling and depth.

As might be expected, the voice of the Living God is a voice of paradox. It is God's voice, and yet it is my voice at the same time. And where it calls the adult self to go seems to be in harmony with what Carl Jung calls "the law of one's own being."[2] The voice of the Living God is a voice of integrity and mutuality, a voice of the self and God together as a unified reality. This voice is variously a voice of vocation, a voice of conscience, a voice of dialogue, and a voice of meaning. It is a voice of spiritual reality, a voice of love, of freedom, and of mystery that the adult self hears in community and in solitude.

SPEAKING TO AND SPEAKING ABOUT
THE LIVING GOD

The adult self in unfettered imaging tends to speak to and to speak about the Living God in terms that are personal, experiential, and figurative. Speech about the Living God is *metaphorical*, and metaphor, says Janet Soskice, is "as satisfying a linguistic form for making truth claims as is literal speech."[3] In those metaphors that are verbally expressed, a given word may have many meanings, and these meanings are relational, contextual, and embodied. The Living God is a God of personal experience, and as Ann and Barry Ulanov put it, "Experience demands metaphor."[4] Metaphor is our language for the Living

God because this God cannot be made objective.[5] The experience of the Living God and our response to that experience is beyond the subject-object dichotomy of reality, in a "place" where only metaphor is spoken.

Metaphor, as understood here, is much more than a clever figure of speech. It is the language of the adult self as an integral self-in-mutuality. It is the language of the body-self because the logic of metaphor is bodily. Marion Woodman says it well: "Metaphor comes out of your bones; it's organic in the body. It resonates and you feel whole."[6] Metaphor is the language of feeling and the language of depth. Metaphor, as artists know, is the language of clear boundaries. Metaphor, as lovers know, is the language of intimacy, and it is the language of the self as its own responsible process. Actualizing and reflecting, which are the relational ways of being of an adult self, are captured and celebrated only in metaphor.

Metaphor is also the language of process and paradox, and it is the language of unfettered imaging, religious experiencing, and mystical knowing.[7] The God as Thou or the Spiritual Reality, the God of Love, the God of Mystery, the God of Freedom, and the God of Community can really be spoken only in metaphor. When the adult self in unfettered imaging speaks *to* the Living God, that is, when this self dwells with the Living God in prayer and in silence, the language is metaphorical. When the adult self speaks *about* the Living God, in whatever way the experiencing of this God is expressed, the language is metaphorical as well.

INTEGRAL SPIRITUALITY

Spirituality can be defined as *that which gives meaning to life and allows us to participate in the larger whole*. Whatever its focus may be, and whether it is religious or not, spirituality is not something "other than" the human, or "transcending" the human, or "added on to" the human. Spirituality is part of our human development, and as such, it comes into its fullness in adulthood. Although we often speak of spirituality as if it were some special "thing," the truth is that the need for meaning and to be part of a larger whole is inherently human. The full-ness of any living spirituality is, and could only be, in harmony with the fullness of the human. The reason, therefore, that we can speak of adult religion as a full or integral spirituality is not, as is often assumed, because religion and spirituality have to go together. Rather, it is be-cause adult religion and integral spirituality are both rooted in adult-hood.[8]

An integral spirituality is found in *an integral self-in-mutuality*. Any integral spirituality calls us to be the wholeness of who we are even as it invites us to relate to some meaningful larger whole or larger reality. "Spirituality is our openness to relationship, which is a universal hu-man capacity involving the whole person."[9] It is "the human quest for personal meaning and mutually fulfilling relationships among people, the nonhuman environment, and for some, God."[10] What is not of the self-in-mutuality is not spirituality. "Whenever we think of ourselves as separate, fear and attachment arise and we grow constricted, defensive, ambitious, and territorial."[11] What is of the self-in-mutuality is spiritu-ality. Spirituality "surrounds us and is in us and in our relationships."[12] Spirituality is always interactive and inclusive. As Parker Palmer ob-serves, "all of reality is active and interactive, a vast web of mutual rela-tionships."[13] Spirituality is an evolving framework of meaning that each of us as an integral self-in-mutuality is able to find.

1. An integral spirituality is in and of the body-self. Unfortunately, a number of traditions in philosophy and theology invite us to believe that spirituality has nothing to do with the body. But if our spirituality is not in dialogue with our body-self, then it cannot be alive in our re-lationships or in the things we care about. "Spirituality involves a dis-cipline of the whole person."[14] For example, a "sense of compassion-ate mutuality with nature" is possible only through a body-self.[15] If our body-self is not at the core of our spirituality, meaning is reduced to idealized concepts, and "the spiritual" finds itself in opposition to "the material." The truth is, there is no meaning that touches who we are and no meaning that relates us to our environment that does not touch all of who we are and draw us forward as whole, embodied selves. The wholeness of a body-self makes an integral spirituality pos-sible. "The human body is the best picture of the human soul."[16]

2. An integral spirituality is rooted and disclosed in feeling. If feeling is "the wholeness of human response to reality"[17] and if feeling "celebrates unity in diversity,"[18] then feeling is at the heart of any integral spirituality. Spirituality "involves emotional and physical aspects of human experience as well as cognitive aspects."[19] It "involves subtle feelings, a bodily sense, and not simply a cognitive belief system."[20] We *feel* the connections the spirituality brings; we *feel* the rightness of what draws us forward as ourselves; we *feel* what relates us in generous mutuality to the larger reality. If, however, our feeling remains disowned or if it is split into "reason" (the objective) and the "emotions" (the subjective), our spirituality remains split as well. We are not able to find a sense of personal connection in our spirituality, and we forestall the furthering of an adult self as an integral self-in-mutuality.

3. An integral spirituality has a sense of depth. The word "spirituality" is, in fact, a "highly useful code word for the depth dimension of human experience."[21] As Eugene Kelly observes, spirituality involves "a deep sense of wholeness"[22] and "a deep sense of connectedness with others."[23] This depth of wholeness and connectedness, which is often claimed in silence and solitude, may be unsettling and challenging, reminding us "that life cannot be encompassed by rationality but extends into an unknown."[24] "No attempt to define 'spirituality' in words," says Homer Jernigan, "can capture all the aspects of mystery that are inevitably involved in 'spiritual' experiences."[25] Spirituality without depth is without heart, without soul, without spirit. It has no power to transform. But a spirituality with "the willingness and the courage to open oneself to mystery"[26] allows for change and growth. "Whatever is spiritual touches us deeply and can transform suffering into learning, enmity into collaboration, and indifference into love."[27]

4. An integral spirituality has its own clear boundaries. Any integral spirituality must have clear boundaries that can be understood and owned by the self. "Much of spiritual life is self-acceptance, maybe all of it. Indeed, in accepting the songs of our life, we can begin to create for ourselves a much deeper and greater identity in which our heart holds all within a space of boundless compassion."[28] Spirituality *permeates* and *transforms* our boundaries; it does not *transcend* them. We are only spiritual as who we are. Even if we have a formal spirituality that comes from an honored tradition, this spirituality must speak to the whole of our experience. An integral spirituality addresses our issues around boundaries and speaks to suffering, guilt, and death in a way that changes us and lets us grow. Spirituality without clear boundaries that fit the clear boundaries of the body-self is at best an imposed, superego spirituality, and it forestalls the furthering of the adult self as an integral self-in-mutuality.

5. *An integral spirituality exists in intimacy.* Just as there can be no integral adulthood without the experience of intimacy, there also can be no integral spirituality without the experience of intimacy. To speak of intimacy is to speak of empathy, openness, and unconditional love. These three qualities are the relational power at the heart of any integral spirituality. In spiritual terms, empathy, openness, and unconditional love are compassion, and without a living compassion, there is no integral spirituality. A spirituality that does not embody compassion is sterile and devoid of life. It can only forestall the furthering of an adult self as an integral self-in-mutuality.

Furthermore, spirituality and sexuality come together in intimacy. As Lynn Rhodes describes it:

> Our love is embodied in our feelings, our passion, and our care. If spirituality loses touch with its roots in sexuality, it loses power to form and influence our deepest selves. When sexuality is separated from spiritual development, it becomes something we use to manipulate, control, and harm what we profess to love. When spirituality is separated from our sexuality, it loses the power of personal connection and becomes lifeless—it cannot move us to passionate care for the world.[29]

6. *An integral spirituality is its own responsible process.* Any integral or whole spirituality is its own path, its own call, and its own justification. It is only in our own response to the other that meaning is found; it is only in our own response to the larger whole that our spirituality holds, deepens, and transforms the self as it relates in mutuality to that larger whole. In the words of a Zen master, "Unless it grows out of yourself, no knowledge is really of value to you: a borrowed plumage never grows."[30] An integral spirituality cannot be justified by something outside of itself, by fear, by force, by promises, by the glowing tes-

tament of others. And yet, paradoxically, an integral spirituality is often experienced as a call to the self from what is other. An integral spirituality calls us to be our own responsible process, even as it calls us to respond to the needs of our world. In spirituality, as Robert Wuthnow finds, "Taking responsibility for oneself, perhaps ironically, goes hand in hand with doing what one can to help others."[31]

An integral spirituality is in *an actualizing self-in-mutuality*. At times the need to be of service, to act with courage, to be compassionate, and to give and receive comfort may be in the forefront, and we find our spirituality is at one with the ways we engage with others in a mutuality of care and justice. We may find our spirituality in taking care of the members of our family, in engaging with others in our work, in aiding those in the community who need our help, in addressing the broader needs of persons and the needs of the ecology, in taking part in personal or communal rituals or in actions on our part that honor virtues such as hope, gratitude, and forgiveness. In the different ways we "go out to the other," we find meaning in our lives, even as we participate in the larger whole. An actualizing self-in-mutuality is a hallmark of integral spirituality.

An integral spirituality belongs to *a reflecting self-in-mutuality*. At times, the need to be present to the body-self in its feeling and its depth may be in the forefront, and we find our spirituality is at one with the ways we engage our lives as a reflecting self-in-mutuality. We may find our spirituality in solitude, in quiet walks in nature, in sexual embrace, in being with friends, in reading and studying, in attending workshops, in different kinds of physical exercise. We may find it in specific practices that allow for reflection, such as different forms of meditation, working with a therapist, a spiritual guide, or a wisdom figure, and taking time apart for personal retreat. We may find our spirituality in personal or communal rituals or in actions on our part that honor virtues such as hope, gratitude, and forgiveness. In the different ways we "come home to ourselves," we find meaning in our lives, even as we participate in the larger whole. A reflecting self-in-mutuality is a hallmark of integral spirituality.

At this point, we are able to see not only that an integral spirituality takes its structure from the structure of an adult self, but we can also see that adulthood and an integral spirituality are intimately connected. They can be thought of, in fact, as a living dialectic, the one nurturing, sustaining, and furthering the other. If adulthood makes an integral spirituality possible for us, an integral spirituality—in whatever form it may actually take—returns the favor. Often, it provides a framework of meaning that helps us keep our adulthood and that deepens and furthers who we are in our adult living. Without some form of spirituality, it seems, the adult self often has a hard time maintaining itself because there is not enough that is meaningful to draw it forward. "We cannot go on indefinitely," observes Dick Westley, "without an identifiable spirituality."[32] Likewise, if the adult self should begin to fall apart or if becoming an adult self should remain beyond reach, sometimes only some form of spirituality can rescue the self and help it become whole.

At this point, we are also able to see that adult religion—especially as described in terms of "religious experiencing"—functions as an integral spirituality. When, in the unfettered imaging of religious experiencing, the adult self finds the Living God, this self is involved in an integral spirituality. In adult religion, *that which gives meaning to life* is the Living God. In adult religion, *to participate in the larger whole* is to dwell in the Living God. The experience of the God as Thou or the Spiritual Reality, the experience of the God of Love, the experience of the God of Mystery, the experience of the God of Freedom, and the experience of the God of Community are celebrations of an integral spirituality, a spirituality that deepens and transforms the self even as it relates the self-in-mutuality to the Living God.

NOTES

1. John W. Glaser, "Conscience and Superego: A Key Distinction," in *Conscience: Theological and Psychological Perspectives*, ed. C. Ellis Nelson, 167–88 (New York: Newman, 1973), 177.

2. Carl G. Jung, "The Development of Personality," chap. 7 in *The Collected Works of C. G. Jung*, vol. 17, *The Development of Personality* (Princeton, NJ: Princeton University Press, 1981), 174.

3. Janet Soskice, "Knowledge and Experience in Science and Religion: Can We Be Realists?" in *Physics, Philosophy, and Theology: Common Quest*

for Understanding, ed. Robert J. Russell, William R. Stoeger, and George V. Coyne (Notre Dame, IN: University of Notre Dame Press and Vatican Observatory, 1988), 175.

4. Ann Ulanov and Barry Ulanov, *Religion and the Unconscious* (Philadelphia: Westminster, 1975), 243.

5. As Christopher Tilley, *Metaphor and Material Culture* (Oxford: Blackwell, 1999), 4, observes, "Metaphor is linked with emotion and subjectivity and opposed to a disinterested and objective understanding."

6. Marion Woodman, "In Her Own Voice: An Interview with Marion Woodman by Anne A. Simpkinson," *Common Boundary* 10, no. 4 (July/August 1992): 27.

7. See Jane Kopas, *Sacred Identity: Exploring a Theology of the Person* (New York: Paulist Press, 1994), 54, who observes, "Metaphors hold together similarity in difference, and allow us to speak of that which lies beyond our full grasp." See also John Dominic Crossan, "Paradox Gives Rise to Metaphor: Paul Ricoeur's Hermeneutics and the Parables of Jesus," *Biblical Research* 24/25 (1979–1980): 20–37.

8. For an understanding of how psychotherapy, spirituality, and religion are related in adulthood, see John J. Shea, "Adulthood—A Missing Perspective: Psychotherapy, Spirituality, and Religion," *American Journal of Pastoral Counseling* 7, no. 1 (2004): 39–65.

9. Urban T. Holmes, *Spirituality for Ministry* (New York: Harper & Row, 1982), 12.

10. Edward R. Canda, "Spirituality, Religious Diversity, and Social Work Practice," *Social Casework* 69, no. 4 (1988): 243.

11. Jack Kornfield, *A Path with Heart: A Guide through the Perils and Promises of Spiritual Life* (New York: Bantam, 1993), 49.

12. Barbara K. Myers, *Young Children and Spirituality* (London: Routledge, 1997), 62.

13. Parker Palmer, *The Active Life: A Spirituality of Work, Creativity, and Caring* (San Francisco: Jossey-Bass, 1990), 52.

14. Constance Leean, "Spiritual and Psychological Life Cycle Tapestry," *Religious Education* 83, no. 1 (Winter 1988): 49.

15. Drew Leder, *The Absent Body* (Chicago: University of Chicago Press, 1990), 164.

16. Ludwig Wittgenstein, *Philosophical Investigations*, trans. G. E. M. Anscombe (Oxford: Blackwell, 1968), 178.

17. James Nelson, *Between Two Gardens: Reflections on Sexuality and Religious Experience* (New York: Pilgrim, 1983), 10.

18. John Heron, *Feeling and Personhood: Psychology in Another Key* (London: Sage, 1992), 93.

19. Homer L. Jernigan, "Spirituality in Older Adults: A Cross-Cultural and Interfaith Perspective," *Pastoral Psychology* 49 (2001): 417.

20. Elfie Hinterkopf, *Integrating Spirituality in Counseling: A Manual for Using the Experiential Focusing Method* (Alexandria, VA: American Counseling Association, 1998), 11.

21. William H. Becker, "Spiritual Struggle in Contemporary America," *Theology Today* 51 (July 1994): 257.

22. Eugene W. Kelly, Jr., *Spirituality and Religion in Counseling and Psychotherapy: Diversity in Theory and Practice* (Alexandria, VA: American Counseling Association, 1995), 89.

23. Kelly, *Spirituality and Religion in Counseling and Psychotherapy*, 92.

24. Kenneth Bragan, *Self and Spirit in the Therapeutic Relationship* (London: Routledge, 1996), 11.

25. Jernigan, "Spirituality in Older Adults," 417.

26. Gerald G. May, *Will and Spirit: A Contemplative Psychology* (San Francisco: Harper & Row, 1982), 32.

27. Christopher Faiver, R. Elliott Ingersoll, Eugene M. O'Brien, and Christopher McNally, *Explorations in Counseling and Spirituality: Philosophical, Practical, and Personal Reflections* (Belmont, CA: Brooks/Cole, 2001), 1.

28. Kornfield, *A Path with Heart*, 47–48.

29. Lynn Rhodes, *Co-Creating: A Feminist Vision of Ministry* (Philadelphia: Westminster, 1987), 64–65.

30. D. T. Suzuki, *Zen Buddhism* (New York: Doubleday, 1956), 97.

31. Robert Wuthnow, *Creative Spirituality: The Way of the Artist* (Berkeley: University of California Press, 2001), 167.

32. Dick Westley, *Redemptive Intimacy: A New Perspective for the Journey to Adult Faith* (Mystic, CT: Twenty-third Publications, 1981), 91.

10

IMAGES OF THE
LIVING GOD

The following pages on images of the Living God come from the stories of those I have interviewed over the past few years. My primary objective in all the interviews was to allow each person to say as clearly as possible how he or she imaged God. The initial question was, again, if you had to say right now how you image God in your life, what would that image be like? According to the response of the interviewee, I asked other questions so that as complete a picture of God as possible could come from each person. All of the stories presented in this chapter are from chronological adults over the age of twenty-five.

Although all of the stories presented in this chapter are of the Living God, they are only a few of all the different versions of this God. They are all, however, stories of love, and of trust, and of freedom, and in all of them, five things in particular can be noticed. First, personal experience is very important in each one of them; this experience does not necessarily have to be dramatic, but it connects the teller of the story directly and unmistakably with the Living God. Second, even though each of these stories is quite personal and quite unique, there is a mutuality of "the self and God together" that characterizes each of them. Third, as we hear the experience of the Living God in these stories, the truth of the lives of each of the storytellers is also somehow revealed. Fourth, the stories told in this chapter are stories of transformation. It seems that to know the Living God is to be changed in some important way. Fifth—and perhaps most important to point out—the stories told in this chapter come from a level of feeling, of depth, and of intimacy that not only reveals the presence of an adult self but that reveals as well the unfettered imaging of God that is religious experiencing. It is the unfettered imaging of religious experiencing that allows these stories to be stories of an integral spirituality. It is the unfettered imaging of religious experiencing in these stories that allows a God as Thou, a God of Love, a God of Mystery, a God of Freedom, and a God of Community to be revealed.

IMAGES OF GOD

Ricardo

Ricardo is a quiet, self-reflective man who is a minister in his church. He was born on one of the islands in the Caribbean, and he has lived most of his life in circumstances of poverty. Along with a younger brother and a younger sister, he was raised for the most part by his mother, a very strong woman who relied on the help of God to see the family through the difficult times. Now in his early forties, Ricardo has worked out a somewhat satisfying relationship with a father who was away for most of his childhood. Now he is feeling at peace with his life. When I asked Ricardo how he imaged God, he spoke with ease and comfort.

I'd say God is my shadow. I say that because I experience Him as part of myself, as the begetter of myself, the creator of myself. And it is like He is always with me, but I can't see Him. He's part of me, and He's that part I cannot see. I know He is there, but only under certain circumstances do I really realize it. Usually I'm alone, not thinking about anything, and then I realize there is something present in myself. I can't name it. I can't see it. But I can feel that there is something present. And it's like something is inviting me, someone is inviting me, to go farther or to find something in Him in order to go farther, and farther than I consciously really want to go.

I'd say that God is a subtle part of myself. There are two parts to myself. There is myself, and then there is that other myself. There is the per-

son I know I am, the person I experience I am, the person I feel I am, the person I think I am. But there is also that other part of myself, that part which I am not always aware of. And from time to time, that other part of myself reveals itself and invites me to go farther than I would consciously want to go. That's why I call it the shadow. I have come to think of God as the shadow. I can't see it, but sometimes I think other people can see it in me. That's the way I view it now. There's me and my shadow.

Sometimes I feel like there are two voices inside, two inner voices that are competing to be heard, and they are challenging each other. One is saying, "You want to do this," and the other one is saying, "This is good, and I think you should do it." It's what I hear sometimes inside, from inside. And while reflecting on those calls from inside, I realize that the first voice, the voice saying, "You do this," is sometimes my own personal, individual voice and my own ambitions, my own desires, my own perceptions of things and of people. And the other voice that is saying, "This is good and I think you should do it," that is what I would call God's voice. Your perceptions, your visions, your world vision, your desires, your aspirations, they are all good, but there's more than that, and it's like a call to open yourself, to open myself, to other people, to bigger or better realities.

It's not . . . it's not a real voice. I say it's a voice, but I don't hear voices. That's only there inside. After that, I realize that one of them is my own pride, my own personal stuff, but the other inner voice is from some . . . someone else. But I have that from inside, the little voice. I hear it from inside myself. That's why I say He is present. He is always present, even though I can't see. And sometimes I can't even . . . I can't even name it. You have some experiences sometimes that you can't even name. And there is an experience that is there, that has left some kind of imprint.

The way we present God in organized religion and the way we experience God in our individual lives is very different. In the beginning there is a profound need in human beings for the conventions of religion. But as time passes the conventions become a reason or a justification for too many things. If someone wants to go by the conventions, I don't have a problem with that. If I feel like going with them, I will, but if I don't feel like going with them, then I don't. God is pure freedom, and that's the kind of freedom we don't like.

We don't know who we are as men and women. The one who really knows who we are is God. We don't really know what we need. The one who really knows these things is God. We teach the things in religion that we know about God, but God is always surprising us. We tend to think out of fear or insecurity, but God leads us to another path and shows us other ways. He does that because He is freedom, and we are not free. So He is pure freedom, and He is our freedom. We need Him to be free, we need to make our own choices, and we need to believe in our own way and not just be conformists. We need to stand on our own, to make a mature choice. The divine and the human, when they meet, they always meet in freedom.

Vince

A married man in his early forties, Vince has two daughters and one son. He holds a very responsible and influential position in the area of human resources. In addition to what he does because of his position, he is also involved in several organizations in his community that help those who are in need. Vince is, as the French say, "comfortable in his own skin," and he has a great sense of humor. I asked him how he images God. After waiting a minute to find the right words, he said:

It's a feeling, and there are images related to it. It's more a feeling. And the image in that feeling that is most comfortable, and which everybody can relate to, is a loving mother. And there are a million images of what that is, you know, the Pietà, the baby in his mother's arms. But that's only as a reflection of a feeling. The feeling is this unconditional, positive regard. And the word that comes is love, but that's not adequate for it. It is that complete sense of peace, of comfortableness, of serenity, which you see reflected in images of young babies with their mothers, babies asleep in their mother's arms, that kind of thing. That's the feeling, and that's the image of who God is for me.

When I was nineteen years old, I drowned. I died. I was gone. They had to crank me back up. It wasn't long, but I was gone. I was swimming back to shore in a wetsuit from a spot that maybe was a hundred to a hundred and fifty yards out. It was against the current, which I didn't know at the time. At one point in the experience, I was two places at once. I could actually see myself, and knowing that I could see myself. So I was in two places, one physical and one not, and it was a really neat experience. It was, like, simultaneous. And then that stopped, and I just kept swimming.

And then at some point, I wasn't swimming. I was blank. There was a memory gap. The people on the shore said I was still swimming. I have no recollection of that piece of it. It was blank. But for some period of many minutes, I continued to swim. I was on some kind of automatic pilot, but I was not conscious. Then, I reached a point where my flipper on my left foot touched something solid, which kind of roused me. And when that happened, I raised my head to look up. I was coming in on the wave on a steep part of the beach. People kind of recognized that something was amiss or something, but they weren't sure, and they were just watching. And when I took in a deep breath, then the wave was coming down. In that second, I swallowed what seemed like half the ocean.

In that second, I was gone. You know, people talk about hearing God, and that's exactly what happened. Something was happening to me that was not so much uncomfortable as unusual. I started going someplace, and I didn't like it, and I was resisting it. And it was like where the immovable object and the irresistible force meet, and the immovable object is your own free will, and the irresistible force is God. I was resisting God. And then this voice came to me which was genderless, but it sounded human in its intent. And I said mentally to myself, "What's going on?" And there was this voice, which was a feeling more than a voice, and it wasn't me. I know that. But it wasn't not me either. And this voice said, "It's okay." This was very different than the out-of-the-body stuff. I can't describe it. It was reassuring. And still I was resisting.

It said a second time, "It's okay." And then, I let go. I couldn't not go anymore. I knew I had control over not going because the first time I said, "I don't want that." It was the fear and the resistance because it seemed foreign to me. But when the second time came, it was the point of the irresistible force of this feeling and the immovable object of my free will. The feeling was irresistible. I let go. I stopped resisting. And the will and the love met together. They became one. And I started traveling through a boundaryless boundary with a lot of imagery, but what I took away from it was, "The universe is reflected in a grain of sand." It's all part of the same thing. The only way I can describe the feeling of the "It's okay" piece is like a baby being in the arms of a very loving mother. It's the image that conveys the feeling. It's the feeling that is all-inclusive and that is always there. God is always with me.

At some point I heard voices, and the voices said, "He must have panicked." These were real voices. And that was the one thing I hadn't done. I almost did, but I didn't. And I said, "No, that's not true." And I thought I responded. I felt like I had responded verbally. And they said, "Yeah, he must have panicked." And I said, "These jerks didn't hear me the first time. Maybe I should speak louder." And then I felt like I was in the middle of a football huddle laying on my back. I slowly became more aware of people around me, and I remember snippets of things. They did CPR because I wasn't breathing, and they got an ambulance. I was in the hospital for three days.

The first day in the hospital, I was just drifting in and out of consciousness. Late the second day, I remember the doctor came in to see me. And he says, "How are you feeling?" And he says, "You know you are a very lucky guy. You could have drowned. It was lucky there were people there who knew CPR." And you know, he kind of gave me this speech. And I said to him, "You know, some really weird things were happening while I was there." And he says, "Don't worry about it, you're okay now." And I carried that, "Don't worry about it, you're okay now," with me for all these years. But the experience would keep coming back, not in a flashback sense, but more in a sense of wonderment. Years later, I would be walking down the street, and I would suddenly stop and say, "What the hell was that? That was real." It never went away.

With my friends and when I went back to college, they thought this was great. I mean, I had drowned. We had one hell of a party. So, there's no idea. There is nothing within any frame of reference into which you can fit this experience. And the doctor saying, "Forget it," like it was a psychological anomaly. And my parents saying, "Oh, thank God, he's okay." And my friends are having a wild party. So, there was no serious piece to this anywhere. No one could hear what happened. And even for me, I wouldn't even think of this for five or six years. Later, at college, I did some recreational drugs, and I had those experiences of that. And my friends would say, "It's hallucinations." And I would say to myself, "No, that wasn't it." And I kept looking for the box I could put my experience in.

This experience is something you haven't asked for, something for which you are not prepared. I was a hell-raising college student, and you are going to come at me with something like this? Forget it. It took ten or fifteen years of going through this process of trying to find something that I could plug it into, and never being able to find it, before I finally realized that that was it. That what happened was really real. And I had the opportunity to talk to one other person who also had a similar experience, and he happened to be a psychiatrist. I listened to his story, and he listened to my story. And I said, "Am I crazy?" He said, "No." And I said, "Are you crazy?" And he said, "No." And now it's something I go back to every day. It's there. It's my anchor.

Now, I do some weird things, some unconventional things, and people say, "Well, that's not right." And I don't listen to them. I get the guidance from God. And I say, "If this is not right, then let me know." Every relationship with God is personal. God doesn't judge. There isn't any judgment. There are horrendous things, but despite the horrendousness, everyone is loved unconditionally. No one is judged. God let's me know how I should act. If all there is, is love, if no matter what you do, you are embraced by God, what is there to worry about? You're there. You're there alone. It's you and God together, and you are the same thing. It's your humanity as a part of God. So I say, "If this isn't right, let me know." And I do know. For me it's visceral. It's a hesitation; it's a double take; it's something intuitive. You feel it.

You know, it's a mystery. The plan is so much bigger than you can see. It's for you now to do what you need to do, in trust, in complete trust. You do what you need to do to keep the love out there. The question always is, is there enough love here? And the question is, what can I do? There is really only one commandment. "Love yourself and love everyone else." If all there is, is the love, and you know it's there, then no matter what you do, it doesn't matter. There's no condemnation. I feel free all the time. I know that I'm part of the whole plan. I don't have to worry. I know that whatever I need, I'll have. Whatever I need to do, I'll be given the capacity. It's a well that never runs dry. Jesus was looked upon as God because he was totally free. Freedom is from God, like oxygen is part of water. God is freedom. It just is.

There's nothing that's not God. The cars, the buildings here in the city. Including things you would not consider attractive. Everything is God. Is all reflected down to the smallest thing, and everything is in it. It's like fractals. God is in fractal stuff. There is this big image. And you cut out one little piece, and the whole thing is still there in that little piece. It's the same with God. All of creation is part of God. God really did create everything, so there is nothing that's not God. I don't go to church. There is nothing there. I think organized religion is dangerous. It's all very narrow. There's so much hate, so much opposition. They all talk about "we," but it's really a "you-me." And it's irrelevant, a distraction from what I know is there. It's baggage.

It's a mystery. It's always unfolding. The mystery is always there. From moment to moment, you never know what's going to be there for you. I'm part of the mystery, and so are you. It's all part of the mystery. The mystery is the fun part that God puts in for your entertainment. In reality, what can anyone do to me? People are not free because they are afraid of what other people can do to them. In the end, in the ultimate moment, are other people going to be there with me? No. I'm there. It's a review of your life. Only you know. Only you are responsible. I am responsible all the time.

I'm thankful for life, and I'm responsible for life. We are on a mission from God. It's the appreciation of the mystery. And it's the trapeze act. It only happens in the letting go. The thing is in the letting go. Then you have the event. Then it happens.

Joe

A good example of how experiences in everyday life reveal the presence of the Living God is from Joe, a married, midlife businessman who is involved in several programs in his church. Joe is a kind and enthusiastic person, very interested in being helpful to other people and very interested in the practice of his religion. Joe is a person with whom I did not do a formal interview. We met at a social gathering, and during our conversation, I mentioned that I was writing a book about people's experiences of God. He told me this story.

I was waiting one afternoon at the back of the bank, and there was this elderly woman—she must have been at least eighty-five years old—and the manager of the bank was trying to explain something to her about a change that the bank needed to make in her account. But she just couldn't grasp what he was saying. He explained it to her at least three times, but she just could not understand why the bank was going to do something different with her money, and she was getting upset. I was next in line, just to the side of the little cubicle where they were, and there were two people waiting behind me. And the manager was talking as loud as he could because she was hard of hearing. And I thought, "Well Joe, this is interesting; this could take a while."

But the manager of the bank was not at all impatient. Again, in very careful steps, which everyone could hear, he explained the procedure to her, and this time she began to understand. And then he went through the whole procedure once more, and this time she actually seemed to get it. At first, I was getting pretty impatient, but as this little drama un-folded, I started to take it in. And I remember saying to myself, "This poor woman is me, at least in a few years." And then I was deeply touched by the whole scene. The manager showed me who we are as sons and daughters of the living God.

Helen

Helen is a single woman in her fifties, a counselor and a spiritual men-tor who works in an agency that serves a number of churches in her lo-cal community. She is religious and generous in a down-to-earth way, helping people with their psychological and spiritual concerns. In the church and in the broader community, she is considered easy to talk to, a person who is caring, nonjudgmental, and with a lot of practical wis-dom. She is constantly helping others, often at the sacrifice of her own needs. I began the interview by asking her how she imaged God.

Right now? Right now, my answer to that is total unconditional love. I'm not sure that's an image, but that is who God is for me. But lately, I have found myself drawn to more feminine images of God, a Mother

God. I found this icon card, and it's a picture of a woman. It's a woman with, like, a world where her womb is, and all this energy flows in and out, just kind of circular energy, so I get the feeling of a flow of energy. But most of the time, my image of God—I don't really think of God in concrete images a lot—is just a lot of silence, just being in the presence, silent presence.

I really need space to pray, I mean timewise. And given my schedule and all, I don't carve out as much time as I need for my own psychological and spiritual health. I'm there taking care of other people and their needs, and I have to take care of my needs too. In the ordinary day-to-day kind of thing, it's usually prayer on the run. I walk and pray, so sometimes I just go for long walks. I get very calm, extremely calm. When I go on retreat, what happens is, as the retreat progresses, I go into very deep prayer.

Last year on retreat, I was sitting by the side of the lake. I didn't care who was watching me. I was totally unselfconscious, which is very different than what I would normally be. And I'd be totally gone, just totally immersed in an absolute knowledge that God was all pervasive and just this incredible feeling of being at one with God. And one thing that stayed with me for this entire year, when I got really stressed out, I would sit down, and this experience of the retreat would come. It was a kind of mantra that said, "Enter the silence and find love, find love to give birth, to give birth to new life."

At the retreat, I went down to the lake one morning. I was watching the sunrise. I'm not usually up at sunrise, but there was this mist rising off the lake, and I remember sitting there thinking, "Where have the particles of water come from? What continents have the particles of water touched? And where have the birds flown? And whose feet and bodies have sat in the same spot over the years, like the Indians and all the ancestors who have walked and sat and prayed here?" That place was very sacred to the Indians. And I was just totally aware that the whole universe was filled with God. And then I just got totally immersed in God, almost like a mystical union kind of thing.

And then, walking back up to the retreat house, I stopped, and I looked at this leaf on a tree, like one leaf out of all these leaves. And I remember thinking, "There's a symphony of grace in every living thing."

And then I thought, "There's a symphony of grace in every living cell." And then for a time it was like the whole world was just filled with the presence of God. So, during this year, when I began to get really stressed out, sometimes I would just—I have this little prayer corner in my house—I would just sit down and remember that moment and become very peaceful, just very centered.

And transforming, very transforming. The experiences on the retreat not only felt transformative, but they have stayed transformative. There have been different times in my life where prayer has really changed me as a person. And I think last year was one of those times. When I came back here, I came back into the situation of the job and everything. There were times when things got really difficult. I'm not saying that I didn't get annoyed and frustrated. And on top of all that, I felt all the annoyance, all the frustration, and all the pain of being a woman in my dear institutional church. And yet, underneath it all, there was the reality that I'm totally and unconditionally loved by God. And there was a real peace.

Faith in some ways is a struggle for me—it's funny because I've been thinking about this. And it's like different layers. There's this whole idea of, you know, the body of faith, and being a member of the church, and the doctrines of the faith, which I sometimes struggle with. But then there's this deep kind of realization that in a sense isn't faith. I have faith in that I believe in God, but in another sense, people could put me on a rack and torture me to death, and I would not give up that I know God exists and that God loves me. But in a sense, this is not faith because it's experiential.

Usually, faith assumes that you're taking a leap in the dark. But if you've taken a leap in the dark and landed in this totally unconditional love of God, then even in periods of darkness—it's not that I don't have periods of darkness—I am aware of God and of what I am doing. Underneath it all, even if I'm struggling with a lot of the surface things, underneath it all, at this moment in my life, there's that certitude that there is a God and that God is the God of total unconditional love.

Whatever faith is, it's more than the institutional beliefs. I believe somewhat in the church, mainly, I think, because that's the place where I've come to know God. But I'm not convinced that the church is the only way to experience God. In fact, I'm definite that it's not. I think that people come to God in many, many ways and experience God in many, many ways. And I don't think that we have a corner market on the truth. I think we have part of the truth. I believe in Jesus Christ, and I believe in the resurrection. I believe very much in the Eucharist, in the real presence of Jesus. I really believe that, and I find that a kind of on-going strength. But some of this other stuff, like women can't be priests, and women are not supposed to speak—it's a load of nonsense. It's a to-tal load of nonsense! And it's a waste of time. I think we spend too much time talking about all these things in the church as if they were the essence, and then we miss the real essence.

I don't believe that God put the plan together. I just don't. I believe that God sets us in motion, so to speak, and walks with us on the jour-ney. But I don't think that God is a manipulator and a controller. I be-lieve there is a lot of freedom. And that's what it means to be human, I think. God wants that for people, freedom to become the best people that we are, to develop our gifts. And I think there are a lot of psychological reasons why people don't do that. Things happen to people, and people just treat each other badly. You know, abusive parents and things like that. And then some things aren't really purposeful, like sickness and different things that happen. Depending on how you work through those issues, you can either become a more healthy and whole person, or you can shrivel up and die. But I think that God wants us to be free, and healthy, and whole.

Now, I'm not one of these people that are ready to give up the Ten Commandments or anything. I certainly think that people need rules of conduct, and I think any society needs rules of conduct. But I think that when a person really knows that they're loved by someone or by God, then that gives a person the freedom to choose to treat others in a simi-lar manner. Ultimately, if all of us knew and experienced this love, then in a sense we would just do the Golden Rule, "Do unto others as you would have them do unto you." That would be our experience, and that's what we would want for other people. The bottom line of all morality is love.

Bob

Bob is an ordained priest in his fifties who comes from a family that was religious "in a normal, traditional kind of way." Bob is very much himself, and he is rather unique. His natural concern for the spiritual welfare of others seems to flow out of his comfortableness with who he is, out of his intuitive sense of what is real, and out of his relationship with God. Twice in his life he has had a very serious illness, and these experiences seem to have made him even more compassionate. I asked Bob how he imaged God. He thought for a minute, and he said:

When I preach, I always describe Jesus as tall and thin, with graying hair and a large bald spot. And they all laugh. They laugh because I am describing myself. And I say to them, "That's how I image God." I'm not doing it in an egocentric way. If you don't see God in the mirror, you've missed God for real. If God says, "I've created you in my image," then you have to believe that. There was a great show on many years ago called "St. Elsewhere," and one of the doctors went to heaven, and he saw God. And it was a great show. God looked exactly like him. And the doctor said, on the show, he says, "He looked exactly like me." And God said, "You were created in my image, and I do look like you." And the doctor says to God, "Well, what about everybody else?" And God says, "Well, they get it too." And that's it. That we are all created in the image of God, but God is more than one image.

God looks like the person in the mirror. God looks like what you look like because you were created in God's image. But obviously, if you looked in the mirror and I looked in the mirror, we'd have different views. That's exactly what it is. God has different reflections. God has shown different reflections of God's self to the world. He shows you your reflection. He shows me my reflection. But together, the whole reflection of God is of the whole world mirror. A good image would be at a dance, those big multimirrored balls they have in some dancehalls. When people stand on different sides of those balls, they see different reflections of the light. God would be those differences in the light, and not something that any one of us can hold onto by ourselves.

I think I always imaged God as a gentle man. God was always a man because, you know, the "Our Father" projected the man image. God was a gentle man who walked with me to talk about my life story. He was always watching over us and guiding us, and gently, you know. God was always there with me. And the image of a father was good because my own father was good. And I could say "Our Father" without any problems, because even though my own father was strict, I never believed that God wanted me to be perfect. Even though I was not perfect, even though I couldn't do everything well, I knew that God loved me. And my grandmother loved me. My grandmother was a faith-filled woman. I knew that. My grandmother loved God. The way my father told me she died was by saying, "Grandma is now with God in heaven." Then I knew somebody that was with God. So, my connection to God now became my grandmother.

Now, all of that was diametrically opposed to what I heard in church. When I was a kid, that same time period, what I heard was that God was a judge, and that God was always condemning. If you do this wrong, if you do that wrong, God will punish you. When I told my family that I was going to become a priest, their first reaction was, "Why do you want to live like that?" And I remember saying to them, "I don't believe their God. I don't believe their God. And I don't believe that what they are saying about God is right. I'm going to reteach all that because I don't want anybody to believe that stuff." And I said, "Because someone's got to change it, and I don't believe that they're preaching the right message." And that's the thing that I do.

I remember in the seventh grade meeting David and becoming friends, and I was saying, "It's not possible that David and I can be such good friends, and, you know, he wouldn't go to heaven because he's Jewish." And he was such a normal kid. I mean, he was just like me. We were good friends. And so, then I started saying, "It can't be right, you know, that God can't be the way the priests were saying. It's just not possible." And I would try to convince David to become a Catholic, and I would realize I was going up the wrong tree. I mean, there was no way. And then I said, "Hey, there's something wrong with this. Why would God be so upset with this?" We needed more room for some better understanding. And that's when I started to think that the priests could be wrong.

I see God in possibilities that most people don't see. I would say many people limit God and then don't look God up. You know, I think God is very much alive in every kind of person, and every kind of walk of life, and every kind of faith and religion. I'm not sure you're going get every priest that's gonna say that, you know. But I see God there. Because God is the whole of creation, and there's no way I'm gonna get a picture of that. So, if I get your piece, and my piece, and his piece, and her piece, then I have a fuller understanding than if we each just have one piece. I believe everybody has a piece of God as a piece in the picture of human nature.

I've been studying Buddhism, which is contrary to my understanding, to stretch me and enable me to see what an entire culture sees about God. That's wonderful. That's a great gift. And that's about inviting us to grow. And I think the Buddhists have a piece of the truth. They don't have the whole truth, but they have a piece. But we have a piece. So, let's share our chips so that we have a fuller understanding of what this God is all about. So, God is constantly inviting us to stretch and to allow us to expand. And the more we expand, the more God can fill. I think it was Saint Theresa who used the image of the thimble and the cup. They're both filled to the capacity, but one is filled more because it's been able to stretch more and it's bigger.

I'm not dependent on God. Being dependent means, like, everything comes from God. You ask God for everything. Every time I have to do something, I have to pray and get an answer. You know, "God said I have to do this, and God said to do that." That's being dependent on God. I'm not sure, but I don't believe God wants us to be dependent in that respect. I think He's saying, "Hey, this is the ballpark. Play ball. Learn how to play ball. And bring your talents, what you know." God is always saying to me, "Go with what you know. What do you know? Then develop that and bring that out." We have to give that to other people, and then they will tell you what they know, and then we'll all know. Then you'll get a better sense of what is going on.

I do pray for things. I do believe that that has a part. But my answers don't always or don't necessarily come when I pray. Because praying is not just to tell God what I need. God knows what I need. But I have to tell me what I need, and I have to become who I am. But unless I become aware of who I am, then I don't know who I am. So, praying or telling

God what I need is really telling me what I need. It's really telling me what's going on within me. That's an aspect of prayer. Most of my prayer is more about adoration than petition. God is total emptying of God's self into another person and giving back and forth, and that's what love is. Love is the give-and-take of your being with another. That's the relationship of the Trinity and of us. That's what prayer is.

God encourages us to change, but at the same time saying that we are loveable and loved the way we are. Like, God is saying, "I want you to become the best Bob you can become, but I love the Bob that's there now. Don't confuse that fact." See, God is constantly calling me to stretch. God is saying, "Bob, there's an aspect of you that needs to grow." You know, "Let's take a look at this." Or, you know, "Why are you afraid, and what's that feel like for you?" And, I say, "I see the fear as this." So, it is a lot of dialogue, there's no doubt about it. I talk with my spiritual director about these things, to keep me grounded. And most of my journal is dialogue. If someone were to read my journal, you'd think that I was nuts. It's a lot of God talk. It's God saying, "Bob, I love you, but move on." And I write letters to God, and God writes to me. I think letters are vehicles for God to speak to us. Are they letters from God? Maybe, maybe not. Are they vehicles for God to speak to us? Absolutely. Absolutely.

I talk to Him like a friend. We sit down. We go for a walk. I'm on my way to a meeting. "Look at that." Or, "Did you see that gorgeous sky or that beautiful this or whatever?" I'm constantly in communication or in conversation with my God. Now, when I say the two of us are sitting there, I cannot see two people sitting there. I mean, I just know He's sitting there, and I know I'm sitting there. I mean, I can't see me, and I can't see Him, but we're both there. So, there's not a guy with the beard, you know. There's a presence, but it's not a concrete image. It's not concrete at all. You just feel like, you know, you're in the presence, and that's something that is measurable, in a sense, because you can feel it, but in another way, prayer isn't measurable at all.

It's a presence. It's not something that can be painted. It can be felt in the heart. It's not an audible voice in your head. I'm not hearing voices. It's like a perception. It's like telepathic. It's my inner voice speaking to me. I hear it in my whole being. I mean my eyes are closed, and I'm there. It's from the whole being. It's not something out there coming in. It's inside. My whole being radiates the feeling that I'm with this person. It's a dance. It's the constant flow of giving and taking, of pain and joy, where there's that dance, the waves that just come back and forth. It's like music. If you are musically experienced, if you have that nature, well, you don't see things when you hear music, but in a way, you do. And you know what the musician is saying. You feel that vibrancy. It's the same thing in prayer, and it's the same thing in a relationship with God because that's what prayer is.

Now, I've had experiences where God talks back, you know. I've had a number of occasions where I wasn't in control of that dialogue. You know, not that I didn't think He was answering before, but this was far more concrete than I had ever experienced. And that's happened a number of times. It doesn't feel like anything different. It only feels like normal prayer, except there are times when you realize that you're not in control of the thought process. I'm sitting there talking to Jesus in my mind, in my body, you know. Then He starts to go off on a tangent and says, "I want to talk about something else. I want to tell you about this." And he takes total control of the conversation. And I say, "Look, I need proof, I need to know that this is really coming from you." And God gives it to me. Always, always, always. God has never not given proof.

The depth of me wants to be with God. The depth of me wants to dance. See, I see God as a dancer, you know. I see the Trinity as a dance. And the depth of me wants to continue to be in that dance, to be in that flow, to be in that adoration, to be in the fire, to be in that spark, to be part of that circle. That's to me what intimacy with God is all about. So, that's what my depth wants. Does my depth always get it? No. In moments, there are great flames, there are great fires, there are great times. But there are moments where that is not there. But my work is my expression of my relationship with God. I want to invite other people into the dance, and I want to teach other people to dance. So, that's why my work is so important.

TRANSFORMATION

From the Superego God to the Living God

TRANSFORMATION AND WHY IT GETS SO LITTLE ATTENTION

TRANSFORMATION

The transformation of adolescing religion into adult religion is easily understood. The transformation is from "The Superego God" to "The Living God." All three elements of the first paradigm need to be transformed into the corresponding elements of the second. That is to say, the adolescing self needs to be transformed into an adult self, fettered imaging needs to be transformed into the unfettered imaging of religious experiencing, and the characteristics of the Superego God need to be transformed into the characteristics of the Living God. Each of these interacting transformations is, of course, part of a living, developmental process, one that has all the starts and stops and blockages, all the twists and turns and detours, that any human process of change and growth easily entails. Let us look briefly at the transformation of these three interacting elements.

In saying that the adolescing self must be transformed into an adult self, we are saying that a self that is still-forming must finally become fully formed and a self that is still-dependent must draw what it needs from its relating to others to be able finally to stand on its own in relating to what is other. In other words, the still-forming, still-dependent, adolescing self must be transformed into an adult self as an integral self-in-mutuality. This transformation of the adolescing self into the adult self is *essential* and *pivotal* for full human development. It is only on the basis of becoming an adult self that unfettered imaging is possible because unfettered imaging is the imaging that comes—and can only consistently come—freely and fully from the adult self.

For fettered imaging to be transformed into the unfettered imaging of religious experiencing, fantasy needs to be drawn from, worked through, and ultimately left behind. Working through fantasy enables our imaging of God to be no longer constricted, or incomplete, or fettered. Likewise, relating in transference needs to be drawn from, worked through, and ultimately left behind. Working through relating in transference enables our relating to God to become fully mutual and no longer in the service of our becoming needs. Lastly, the logic of objective knowing needs to be drawn from, worked through, and ultimately left behind. Working through the logic of objective knowing enables us to grasp the reality of God not just in concepts but also in terms of felt personal meaning. It is only on the basis of unfettered imaging that we can image the reality of the Living God in an ongoing, consistent, and fully mutual way.

Finally, the Superego God needs to be transformed into the Living God. That is to say, the Supreme Being needs to be transformed into a God as Thou or into a Spiritual Reality. The God of Law needs to be transformed into the God of Love. The God of Belief needs to be transformed into the God of Mystery. The God of Dependency and Control needs to be transformed into the God of Freedom. And the God of the Group needs to be transformed into the God of Community. *The experience of the Living God in a consistent and ongoing way is the hallmark of adult religion.*

WHY TRANSFORMATION GETS SO LITTLE ATTENTION

While it is easy enough to understand what is entailed in the transformation of adolescing religion into adult religion, it may be harder to understand why this transformation is so little appreciated. Why does adult religion—the fullness of religion, the fullness of "the self and

God together"—get so little attention, on the personal level, on the societal or cultural level, and within organized religion? The answer to this question lies, I believe, in several general and rather practical reasons, two on the personal level and one on the cultural level.

A reason, on the personal level, why transforming adolescing religion gets so little attention is that many of us are quite happy with the Superego God. The Superego God is simply what we presume God to be. If there are some contradictions in this God, and even if we have some ambivalent feeling and conflict with this God, there is no reason at all to suppose that there is something wrong with God or even with the way we image God. The thinking is that God is what we know God is. The Supreme Being does not change. Religion is not had in different paradigms. If anything needs to change in religion, it is ourselves. We need to be better religious people. We need to follow the law more closely. We need to act more morally. We need to believe more firmly in the power of God. The heart of religion is, and has always been, in adherence to the Superego God. This is what religion is. It could not possibly be anything other than this.

Another reason, on the personal level, why transforming adolescing religion gets so little attention is that the transformation of adolescing religion into adult religion is often very challenging, even if the importance of this transformation can be clearly felt and understood. We may not be all that happy with how we have grown or with the person we have become. We also may not be all that happy with who God is for us or with our imaging of God. But then, knowing that it is possible for us to be different and that it is possible for our imaging of God to be different may be difficult for us to realize. And then, finding a way to allow ourselves and our relationship with God to change is still another problem. Transformation often takes a considerable amount of personal courage, along with conscious effort, the willingness to be challenged, and a sustained commitment to finding something more adequate, more authentic, and more life giving.

A reason, on the cultural level, why transforming adolescing religion gets so little attention is that our efforts at transformation often receive very little support, not just from the society but often from organized religion as well. In many ways, in fact, adult religion is countercultural. There is, unfortunately, little context either within the culture or within organized religion for pursuing religion in terms that are anything more than conventional or formal. Before we look, in chapter 12, at some of the specific things that hinder the advent of adult religion, it may be helpful to look at three explanations of why this issue of the transformation of superego religion into adult religion gets so little hearing on the cultural level and in organized religion.

First, with the rise of modern science in the seventeenth century and with the logic of objective knowing that came with it, religion became hostage in a new way to the subject-object dichotomy of reality.[1] In this dichotomy, religion is not about "the self and God together." Rather, religion is about God. The person is simply not included in the definition. Once God alone is the object of religion, it is easy to see how this God comes to be seen as "other" than us, as very distant, as objectlike, and as immensely powerful. As the self disappears, God becomes a Supreme Being. A developmental and relational perspective, which religion as "the self and God together" requires, is completely lost. In this dichotomized religion, a fixed Superego God, a God that is thought to be "eternal" and "immutable," is all that can be considered. To think of religion as something that might need to undergo transformation makes no sense at all.[2]

Second, in social-scientific approaches to religion, it has become commonplace to study the self along with society and culture and to leave God in brackets. Religion is understood as the study of the self and [God], whatever status or meaning [God] may have.[3] This approach is taken, in part, because the reality of God is questionable in a logic of objective knowing and because it is hard to know how much, if not all, of the God that we have is the product of fantasy and relating in transference. In religion, therefore, not only does the subject-object dichotomy of reality separate the self from God, but it also separates God from the self. That is, this dichotomy casts doubt on our ability to experience God and on our ability to speak about our experience.[4] As we have seen, the subject-object dichotomy turns God into an object, a Supreme Being, a static Superego God. Why should we be concerned about transforming a static Superego God that is beyond our experience and that we suspect may be nothing more than the product of our own fantasy, relating in transference, and logic of objective knowing?

Third, in organized religion, a great deal of the education that takes place is concerned with teaching adolescing selves about God. Whatever the intention of those who engage in this teaching, adolescing selves who are still-forming and still-dependent are going to find, for the most part, some version of the Superego God. Organized religion becomes the conveyor, if not the champion, of the Supreme Being, of the God of Law, of the God of Belief, of the God of Dependency and Control, and of the God of the Group. If religion is understood by adolescing selves as facts to be known about God and as rules set forth by God, it is hard to see how it could be anything other than fixed and unchangeable. What could be more fixed and unchangeable than the laws of an "eternal" and "immutable" God? Furthermore, if the custodians of organized religion have little or no religious experiencing, if they also understand religion as a set of facts about God and as rules given to us by God, then the language of transformation can remain forever unspoken in organized religion.[5]

NOTES

1. See Scott Peck, "Matter and Spirit," in *Further along the Road Less Traveled: The Unending Journey toward Spiritual Growth* (New York: Simon & Schuster, 1993), 175–93, for an interesting description of how this happened historically.

2. I do not mean to suggest that there is not a long history of the subject-object dichotomy in different philosophical and theological understandings of God. Jerry H. Gill, *Mediated Transcendence: A Postmodern Reflection* (Macon, GA: Mercer University Press, 1989), 147, refers to "the standard epistemological dualism that has plagued philosophy almost from its inception, namely that between the knowing subject and the known object." The logic of objective knowing, which still strongly influences both theology and the philosophy of religion, was simply recast and validated with the rise of modern science.

3. For an exception to this approach, see Moshe H. Spero, *Religious Objects as Psychological Structures: A Critical Integration of Object Relations*

Theory, Psychotherapy, and Judaism (Chicago: University of Chicago Press, 1992).

4. The subject-object dichotomy of reality has split the notions of both "experience" and "religious experience," making them either something "objective," having to do with empirical evidence, or something "subjective," having to do with feelings and emotions.

5. For a writer who is both passionate and eloquent on this point, see Abraham H. Maslow, *Religions, Values, Peak Experiences* (New York: Viking Compass, 1970).

12

WHAT HINDERS TRANSFORMATION

To consider the specific things that hinder the transformation of adolescing religion into adult religion is to raise another set of three questions. The first question is, what things hinder the transformation of the adolescing self into the adult self? As we have seen, the adult self, with the unfettered imaging that comes from it, is essential and pivotal for a consistent imaging of the Living God. In other words, adulthood is essentially a religious issue. The truth is that *whatever hinders the adult self hinders the Living God.*

The second question is, what things hinder the transformation of fettered imaging into unfettered imaging? In other words, what keeps fantasy, relating in transference, and the logic of objective knowing from being transformed into the unfettered imaging of religious experiencing? And the third question is, what things hinder the transformation of the characteristics of the Superego God into those of the Living God? Unfortunately, even if we are functioning as adult selves with unfettered imaging, we may still find it very difficult to image a Living God.

These three questions reflect, of course, the central questions with which this research began: *Why is our relating to God so often presented as if it were something static and not something meant to develop as we ourselves develop and mature?* Therefore, *why are so many adults still living with a God of childhood and adolescence, a Superego God?*

THINGS THAT HINDER THE ADULT SELF

The things that hinder the adult self are simply the things that keep us from becoming an integral self-in-mutuality. They are the things that keep us from being a body-self with its feeling and its depth, its intimacy with clear boundaries, and its own responsible process. And they are the things that keep us from adult actualizing and reflecting. Some of these things are captured here under five headings.

1. *A lack of love, nurture, respect, and affirmation in the formative years of life.* Insufficient love, nurture, respect, and affirmation in the formative years of life can hinder the adult self. Few of us, it seems, are able to get everything we need as we are growing up.

> Human beings are not born fully formed—like the biblical Adam and Eve. Rather, humans are born as vulnerable infants—needing hands to catch them, arms to hold them, breasts to feed them, and eyes to see them. Human beings need help to grow into the fullness of their human possibility—to learn who they are, what they feel, what they need, and what they can offer the world. They need to be loved and to have others accept and value their love for them.[1]

It is not just that parents are not perfect. It is also that most families have major difficulties of some kind to contend with—illness, separation, only one parent, lack of resources, various kinds of conflict, the demands of work, and a host of other problems and stresses. Some of us experienced neglect, or abuse, or violence of one kind or another. Some of us were spoiled or were too sheltered or protected. Some of us were loaded with family, or societal, or cultural expectations that were either stifling or impossible for us to realize. Some of us received negative messages about ourselves that cut deeply into our confidence and initiative.

The truth is that normal development is not normal. Satisfaction of the basic needs that Abraham Maslow speaks of as necessary for development—the physiological needs, the security needs, the love and belonging needs, and the esteem needs—is easily thwarted. The impediments to development that Erik Erikson speaks of—too much mistrust, too much shame and doubt, too much guilt, too much inferiority, and too much confusion of identity—are easily come by. The self that is still-forming and still-dependent often has a hard time of it. Chronological adulthood is no guarantee of real adulthood.

2. *The addictions, the dependencies, and what others may think of us.* If we are suffering from one or more of the addictions, we are continually trying to "fix" ourselves by using mind-altering and mood-altering substances, activities, possessions, other persons, or even religious convictions and practices to avoid what we are actually feeling. At the same time, we are usually isolating ourselves since we are substituting these things for personal relationships and intimacy.[2] The tragedy of the addictions is that they arrest and then regress the development of the self as an integral self-in-mutuality. They destroy the body-self in its feeling and in its depth, in its boundaries and its intimacy, and in the becoming of its own responsible process. The addictions make adult actualizing and reflecting virtually impossible.[3]

If we are suffering from the dependencies, we also find it very difficult to realize the adult self. Issues around boundaries and responsibility are especially hard. We rely on someone else for our sense of identity, and we make someone else responsible for our welfare. We may be highly invested in caring for others at the expense of caring for ourselves, or we may be highly invested in controlling the lives of others because our own lives are without direction and out of control.

If we are suffering from what others may think of us, we usually end up not paying much attention to the needs of the body-self, or to what we are feeling, or to the desires and intimations that come from the depth because we are afraid we will not be accepted or thought well of by others. We may try to deny our boundaries and our real needs for intimacy, and we may act as if we are not our own responsibility. The addictions, the dependencies, and what others may think of us hinder the adult self because in depleting the self and failing to respect its needs, they make it impossible to live as an integral self-in-mutuality.

3. *Some experiences of suffering, trauma, and loss.* Many of us experience significant suffering or loss of some kind. We may be seriously ill, or we may have had some serious problems as a child. We may have lost a mother, or a father, or a sister, or a brother. Perhaps our parents separated or divorced. Perhaps we never even knew our father or our mother. For

some of us, something traumatic may have happened that turned the world upside down, and we have never been the same. The suffering, the loss, or the trauma may have devastated us, freezing us in disbelief at the time when the terrible event took place. Life continued on somehow, but we stopped living. Perhaps, we never felt safe enough to be with the pain and to try to come to some understanding of the loss.[4]

4. Societal and cultural constraints, including racism, classism, ageism, and sexism. If our society will not allow us the opportunity to become an adult self and if the culture will not support our efforts in this direction, it can be very difficult for us to achieve adulthood. Opportunities to "love and work" may be meager or hard to find. There may be various pressures that make marriage and the raising of children problematic. Good education and vocational training may not be accessible. Appropriate work may simply not be available. In addition, how the culture—especially the popular culture as reflected in the media and in advertising—looks at adults and what the culture proposes as appropriate norms for loving and working may have little to do with our actual needs in living as an integral self-in-mutuality.

If we suffer from a disability, we may be seen by others as less than worthy of human dignity and respect. If we suffer from racism, we are made to be inferior or invisible because of our ethnic background or the color of our skin. If we suffer from classism, we are made to be less as persons because we are part of a devalued group. If we suffer from ageism, we are made to be less as persons because of our age. If we suffer from sexism, we are made to be inferior as human beings simply on the basis of our gender or sexual orientation. In all of these "isms," our full personhood is denied by others, and often the things needed for growth are withheld or made barely accessible. These "isms" directly attack our integrity as persons and our ability to relate in mutuality.

Particularly insidious and destructive is the patriarchal nature of the culture, along with the patriarchal structure of organized religion within the culture. Patriarchy attacks women in their adult selves and in their relating to God at the same time. And because patriarchal structures can make it very difficult for women to be heard as adult and as religious, these same structures can also make it very difficult for men to speak as adult and as religious.[5] The truth is that integrity of the self and mutuality with the other are, and can only be, two sides of the same coin. "Mutuality means not only that men speak and women hear, but that women also speak and men hear."[6] Patriarchal structures are a disaster for the adult self, and they are a disaster for adult religion.

5. *Inadequate life choices and sinful responses.* We may suffer from life choices we have made but do not know how to live with, or recover from, or move on from. Some life choices turn out to be poor choices, choices not clearly thought out perhaps, or choices made for the wrong reasons. Some life choices were good choices at the time, but they simply did not work out the way we had expected. Often these inadequate life choices, which mostly have to do with either love or work, leave us stuck with no way to move forward.[7] These choices do not fit the body-self in its feeling and its depth, or in its need for clear boundaries and intimacy, or in its need to be a responsible process. For some of us, inadequate life choices keep us from becoming an adult self.

Although sin is what we do deliberately to impede the mutuality of "the self and God together," sin is also whatever we do to ourselves or to others that deliberately puts some kind of block in the way of the adult self.[8] Sin has a defiant, "I can, but I won't" quality to it. We sin when we are really able to act responsibly and when the situation call us to act responsibly, and still we choose not to. Sin blocks "the relational grain of existence."[9] Sin actively denies the self as an integral self-in-mutuality. It actively denies the body-self with its feeling and its depth. It actively refuses to honor boundaries and to respect intimacy. It actively denies the self as a responsible process. Sin is actively choosing not to live as an actualizing and reflecting adult self. We sin when the time comes when we are really able to do the right thing to allow ourselves and others to change and grow, but we still do not do it. We sin whenever we act in freely and deliberately chosen ways to impede, or burden, or diminish the self that is wanting to unfold.

THINGS THAT HINDER UNFETTERED IMAGING

All the things, of course, that hinder the adult self are the things that also hinder unfettered imaging, because unfettered or integral imaging is, as we have seen, the imaging that naturally flows from the adult self. Still, it may be helpful to look separately at the "staying power" of fantasy, relating in transference, and the logic of objective knowing in religion, not only because these are the three central strands of fettered imaging that need to be transformed into the unfettered imaging of religious experiencing, but also because these three strands of imaging are often so influential in themselves that they can keep us stuck in adolescing religion even when we are adult in the other areas of our lives.

The Staying Power of Fantasy

The staying power of fantasy in religion is not hard to understand. It comes basically from the power of the adolescing self's needs and wants and from the power vested in the Superego God to satisfy these needs and wants. Three things conspire to make our early imaging of God so significant and, ultimately, so difficult to transform. First, the beginnings of our early imaging of God, especially around the ages of three, and four, and five, occur at a time when our fears and our fantasies are incredibly unbridled and alive, able to make things, including the Superego God, wonderfully unbridled and alive as well.

Second, and at the same time, our early experiences of God are often closely tied to our experiences of our parents. The longing we have for love and care from God may reflect the longing we have for love and care from our parents. The bond and the nurturance we have with God may go hand in hand with the kind of bond and nurturance we have with our parents. The beliefs and values we begin to develop about God may be strongly influenced by the beliefs and values our parents live by. Our response to the way our parents are with us—often with wonderfully elemental feelings of love and trust, fear and conflict, guilt and defiance—easily becomes one with our response to God.[10]

Third, and at the same time, our own smallness and vulnerability help to measure the size and the mighty power of God. In fact, the tiny self and the almighty God really define each other, setting out the identities of both and laying the foundation of "the self and God together," as it is found in the paradigm of "The Superego God."

The Superego God, therefore, comes to us so early in life, is so elaborated in fantasy, is so much involved in our elemental feelings about our parents, is so much in terms of our own smallness and vulnerability, and is so intimately connected with our emerging sense of who we are and how the world is, that to question the reality of this God could hardly cross our minds.

As we continue to grow, three additional factors help keep our fantasy of the Superego God in place. First, we are not able, of course, to engage and interact concretely with the Superego God the way we can concretely engage and interact with our parents, our teachers, and others in the community. Second, we may soon find ourselves in a culture, and perhaps in an organized religion, that only seems to know and reinforce imaging of a Superego God. Third, we may hear God described only in formal terms; we may rarely, if ever, hear anyone we trust speak of God in terms of a personal relationship that seems to be genuine. Therefore, even if we begin to experience some of the contradictions in the Superego God and even if, surprisingly enough, we have significant experiences of a Living God, it may still take a great deal of courage, sustained conscious effort, and ongoing support from others to begin letting the Superego God become transformed.

The Staying Power of Relating in Transference

Because fantasy and relating in transference go hand in hand in adolescing religion, the staying power of our transference relationship with God is easily understood. In Freud's thinking, in fact, this transference relationship was seen as something we would never outgrow:

> As we already know, the terrifying impression of helplessness in childhood aroused the need for protection—for protection through love—which was provided by the father; and the recognition that this helplessness lasts throughout life made it necessary to cling to the existence of a father, but this time a more powerful one.[11]

The all-powerful God, especially early in the telling, seems able to do anything, in terms of safety and protection, in terms of providing for all the things that we need, and in terms of giving us caring adults whom we can love and who will love us in return. Although these needs are transformed as we get closer to appropriating an adult self, they are so strong and so constitutive of the beginnings of "the self and God together" that to work through our relating in transference may be nearly impossible—whether we feel the Superego God has provided for us or not. Allowing our relationship with the Superego God to become transformed can be a terribly confusing, wrenching, and disillusioning experience, one that evokes feelings of fear, anxiety, guilt, loss, vulnerability, ingratitude, betrayal, and abandonment.

Working through our transference relationship with the Superego God is all the more difficult, of course, because, as it turns out, this God often seems to have not the slightest interest in being transformed. The truth is that the Superego God has as hard a time growing up as we do. The Supreme Being does not take kindly to losing its place of preeminence and power. The God of Law does not take kindly to being reasoned with. The God of Belief does not take kindly to our looking for more personal depth in the relationship. The God of Dependency and Control does not take kindly to our acting on our own initiative. The God of the Group is not at all pleased when we try to relate in mutuality or try to make sense of our own experience. Once the Superego God is solidly enthroned, once this God has become part and parcel of who we are, once we relate as naturally to this God as we relate to ourselves, our understanding of this deity is often exceedingly hard to change, even for a self who is adult in every other way.

The Staying Power of the Logic of Objective Knowing

Finally, the staying power of the logic of objective knowing in religion is not hard to understand. In adolescing religion, this logic tends to work in two clear yet slightly different ways. In the first way it works, this logic holds that God is understood in empirical and objective terms. It leaves us to conclude either that God is real, based on what we believe to be empirical and objective criteria, or that God is not real, again based on the same criteria. In the second way it works, a somewhat indirect way favored by many philosophers of religion and theologians, this logic holds that God is *beyond* the empirical and the objective in a *transcendent* realm that we can somehow know about but that we cannot directly experience.[12] Although the second way is more subtle than the first, its logic is still the same. Either way, therefore, we remain locked in a subject-object dichotomy of reality that can reveal only the Supreme Being, the Superego God.

The logic of objective knowing is so much a part of most cultures, so much a foundation of modern science, and so much an assumption in organized religion that for all practical purposes, this logic is never confronted. With its wonderful predictability and control, this logic is the hallmark of mature thinking in the West. To question the adequacy of this logic is to be thought of as either simpleminded or irrational. The truth is, however, that while the logic of objective knowing does allow some of us to hold on to a Superego God, this logic renders any transformation of this God outside the realm of possibility, even for an adult self. In religion, the logic of objective knowing and an integral self-in-mutuality with God cannot go together.

THINGS THAT HINDER THE LIVING GOD

In addition to all the things that hinder the adult self and unfettered imaging, there may be a number of things that the Superego God does for us on a personal level that make it hard for us to let this God be transformed into the Living God. The Superego God may, for example, be a God of Habit for us, a God we have grown accustomed to have in a certain way. Or the Superego God may be a God of Convention for us, making God a common assumption and a convenient reference for our lives. Or the Superego God may a God of Fear for us, leaving us very afraid to question, lest we be punished for our impiety. However, of all the different reasons why we might want to hold onto the Superego God, even when we really know better, two overall reasons are, for many of us at least, especially important.

1. *Needing to control God.* Because the Superego God is so powerful and because this God holds out the promise of getting us what

we need and want, we have a hard time letting this God go. Our hope is to control how God thinks and acts so that we can be safe and secure and so that we can get what is important to us in life. We defer to the Supreme Being. We obey the God of Law. We conform to the God of Belief. We go along with the God of Dependency and Control. We adhere to the God of the Group. And because this all-powerful Superego God can also be quite terrifying, especially if we have not been conforming very well, we may try to keep this God at a great distance from us so that we do not have to deal with this God at all. Holding on to the illusion that we can control life, including holding on to the illusion that we can control God, is often a very difficult thing to work through and to let go of, even for an adult self.[13]

2. *Needing to hold God accountable.* The other side of needing to control God seems to be needing to hold God accountable. We hold on to the Superego God because we can hold this God liable for what happens to us and to what we care about. We can hold this God responsible for the hand that we have been dealt in life. We can be angry with this God for what this God has allowed to happen to us and to our loved ones. We can blame this God for our weaknesses and our vulnerabilities, especially for the pain and suffering we endure, for the shame and guilt we experience, and for the death that we all must face. We can charge this God with complicity for all the misfortune and evil that exists in the world. We hold on to the Superego God because we have unfinished business with this God. Holding on to a God we can hold accountable is often a very difficult thing to work through and to let go of, even for an adult self.

In addition to whatever personal reasons we might have for holding onto the Superego God, if we belong to an organized religion, we may have further cause to remain with this God. If it is quite true that organized religion can help us to experience the Living God, it is also quite true that it can hinder the experience of this God. Three ways that organized religion may hinder our ability to experience of the Living God are mentioned here. Viktor Frankl calls these the "three stumbling blocks," which account for much of the repression that occurs in religion: authoritarianism, rationalism, and anthropomorphism.[14]

Authoritarianism

Organized religion can easily become authoritarian. Once the power of the Superego God is vested in the religious leadership, this leadership—which is somehow Godlike and almost always male—reveals to us in clear and unmistakable terms what God is thinking and feeling about certain issues, why God is acting in a certain way, how we must understand God, and what we must do to be acceptable to God. On the one hand, authoritarianism in religion treats us as adolescing selves who need to be controlled. On the other hand, it tends to offer us human dictates in place of a relationship with the Living God.

Authoritarianism has many faces in religion. One face is an exaggeration of one or more of the characteristics of the Superego God (for example, law, or belief, or dependency, or control). Another face is a continuous focus on guilt (for example, always pointing to the ways we fall short). Another face is the use of power and fear by the leadership to enforce the obedient behavior of the membership (for example, silencing, shaming, and expelling members). Another face is a hierarchical structure of leadership (for example, clearly empowering some and disempowering others). Another face is stereotyped gender roles (for example, what women, because they are women, and men, because they are men, are allowed or not allowed to do).

Another face of authoritarianism in religion is only allowing literal interpretations of sacred texts (for example, only one literal meaning of the text is acceptable). Another face is the love of dichotomies (for example, us and them, good and evil, sacred and secular, the saved and the damned). And still another face is boundary confusion around money, sex, and power (for example, the prevalence of abuse and scandal).[15] To the extent that an adult self is committed to an organized religion and to the extent that this religion is authoritarian, access to the Living God is made difficult, if not impossible. A God as Thou or Spiritual Reality, a God of Love, a God of Mystery, a God of Freedom, and a God of Community cannot be revealed in authoritarian religion.

Rationalism

Rationalism in organized religion is the understanding that God can be grasped by reason alone. With deep roots in the logic of objective knowing, rationalism suggests that religious facts are objective and that religious beliefs, if they cannot be reasoned to directly, are at least reasonable and make good sense. Subtle as it is simple, rationalism presents religion as something of the mind, something to be grasped by an intellectual assent, something clear, objective, and able to be contained and controlled by concepts. The adult self as an integral self-in-mutuality, the body-self, the self as feeling, the self as depth, never has to be engaged; the wholeness of human relatedness and response can be conveniently bypassed.[16]

What we get with rationalism in organized religion is a flat, two-dimensional God, a superficial God, a God without feeling, and a God without depth. What we get is a God of Reason, a God of Logic, a God of Concepts, and a God of Belief. If we can find only rationalism in our organized religion, we may have a very hard time experiencing the Living God in that setting, even if we are adult selves. A God as Thou or Spiritual Reality, a God of Love, a God of Mystery, a God of Freedom, and a God of Community cannot be revealed in rationalistic religion.

Anthropomorphism

An organized religion becomes anthropomorphic when its God is in all-too-human form. This anthropomorphism, which has its roots in fantasy, relating in transference, and the logic of objective knowing, makes not only for a Superego God who is very much as we are—thinking as we do, feeling as we do, and acting and reacting as we do—but unfortunately, this anthropomorphism also makes for a God who has some of our worst characteristics. This God may be filled with hatred, or revenge, or prejudice, or righteousness. This God may be withholding, cruel, condemning, intolerant, tyrannical, and perfectionistic.

Much too small and mean-spirited, an anthropomorphic God easily renders our religion much too small and mean-spirited. In fact, this God often winds up in the service of an authoritarian agenda of power, fear, and control. An adult self who has experienced the confusion and divisiveness that an anthropomorphic God brings to organized religion may never recover from the damage that has been done. Access to the Living God may be blocked forever. A God as Thou or Spiritual Reality, a God of Love, a God of Mystery, a God of Freedom, and a God of Community cannot be revealed in anthropomorphic religion.

NOTES

1. Susan L. Nelson, "Soul-Loss and Sin: A Dance of Alienation," in *On Losing the Soul: Essays in the Social Psychology of Religion*, ed. Richard K. Fenn and Donald Capps (Albany: State University of New York Press, 1995), 100.

2. Craig Nakken, *The Addictive Personality: Understanding Compulsion in Our Lives* (New York: HarperCollins, 1988). See Leo Booth, *When God Becomes a Drug: Breaking the Chains of Religious Addiction and Abuse* (Los Angeles: Tarcher, 1991).

3. John J. Shea, "The Impact of Chemical Addiction on the Realization of an Adult Self" (unpublished study, Fordham University, 1997).

4. See Judith L. Herman, *Trauma and Recovery* (New York: Basic Books, 1992).

5. Robert Moore and Douglas Gillette, *King, Warrior, Magician, Lover: Rediscovering the Archetypes of the Mature Masculine* (San Francisco: HarperSanFrancisco, 1990), xvii, state, "In our view, patriarchy is *not* the expression of deep and rooted masculinity, for truly deep and rooted masculinity is *not* abusive. Patriarchy is the expression of the *immature* masculine." The authors go on to say, "Patriarchy, in our view, is an attack on *masculinity* in its fullness as well as femininity in its fullness. Those caught up in the structures and dynamics of patriarchy seek to dominate not only women but men as well. Patriarchy is based on fear—the boy's fear, the immature masculine's fear—of women to be sure, but also fear of men."

6. Eugene C. Bianchi and Rosemary R. Ruether, *From Machismo to Mutuality: Essays on Sexism and Man-Woman Liberation* (New York: Paulist Press, 1976), 84.

7. For a thoughtful book on life choices, see Tod Sloan, *Life Choices: Understanding Dilemmas and Decisions* (Boulder, CO: Westview, 1996).

8. See Jane Kopas, "Sin and Creaturely Identity," *Sacred Identity: Exploring a Theology of the Person* (New York: Paulist Press, 1994), 168–90.

9. Mary Grey, "Falling into Freedom: Searching for a New Interpretation of Sin in a Secular Society," *Scottish Journal of Theology* 47, no. 2 (1994): 240. For a developmental and relational understanding of sin, see also Nelson, "Soul-Loss and Sin."

10. See Ana-Maria Rizzuto, *The Birth of the Living God* (Chicago: University of Chicago Press, 1979), 31, where, viewing these early years of childhood from an object relations point of view, she says that the "oedipal complex, the formation of the superego, and the formation of the inner world eventuate a final psychological process, namely, the transmutation of the parental imago into the God image."

11. Sigmund Freud, *The Future of an Illusion* (Garden City, NY: Anchor, 1964), 47.

12. Harold H. Oliver, *Relatedness: Essays in Metaphysics and Theology* (Macon, GA: Mercer University Press, 1984), 69, observes, "We are so accustomed to reading experience through Kant's eyes that it seldom occurs to us to think of it differently."

13. See Peter A. Campbell and Edwin M. McMahon, *Bio-Spirituality: Focusing as a Way to Grow*, 2nd ed. (Chicago: Loyola Press, 1997), for a clear description of how control gets in the way of spirituality.

14. Viktor E. Frankl, *The Will to Meaning: Foundations and Applications of Logotherapy* (New York: New American Library, 1969), 149. The description of these "three stumbling blocks" is my own.

15. Two different observations can be made here. First, as Nicholas Lash, "Incarnate and Determinate Freedom," in *On Freedom*, ed. Leroy S. Rouner (Notre Dame, IN: University of Notre Dame Press, 1989), 20, observes, "Religion undisciplined by wisdom is as destructive as sexual activity undisciplined by love." Second, the Superego God, because it is objectlike, can be marketed. Anthropomorphic organized religion and marketing of one kind or another seem to go together. Interestingly enough, the Living God cannot be marketed.

16. It is a fundamental mistake to understand reason as disembodied in the first place. George Lakoff and Mark Johnson, *Philosophy in the Flesh: The Embodied Mind and Its Challenge to Western Thought* (New York: Basic Books, 1999), 4, observe, "Reason is not disembodied, as the tradition has largely held, but arises from the nature of our brains, bodies, and bodily experience. This is not just the innocuous and obvious claim that we need a body to reason; rather, it is the striking claim that the very structure of reason itself comes from the details of our embodiment."

13

WHAT FACILITATES TRANSFORMATION

If we ask what facilitates the transformation of the paradigm of "The Superego God" into the paradigm of "The Living God," the immediate answer is, of course, quite clear. It is whatever facilitates the transformation of the adolescing self into the adult self. It is whatever facilitates the transformation of fettered imaging into the unfettered imaging of religious experiencing. And it is whatever facilitates the transformation of the Superego God into the Living God. In this chapter, we look briefly at some of the ways these facilitations can occur.

THINGS THAT FACILITATE THE ADULT SELF

The things that facilitate the adult self are, for the most part, things that address the lack, or deficiency, or inappropriateness that hindered the development of this self in the first place. Some of these things are considered here under five headings.

1. Love, nurture, respect, and affirmation. When we have not received the love, the nurture, the respect, and the affirmation we needed while we were growing up, we may keep looking for these things, or we may act as if we received them, or we may simply give up hope of finding them. The truth is, however, that nothing really substitutes for love, nurture, respect, and affirmation. The experience of these precious human qualities is essential for our growth and becoming. They are for the self what nourishing food is for the body, and their absence leaves an emptiness and a hunger that is painful and that may have us responding to life with hesitancy, resentment, envy, anger, and defensiveness.

For some of us, the support of friends, or family members, or mentors, or teachers, or coworkers may offer us what we need. For some of us, a counselor or a psychotherapist may provide the kind of honest, caring relationship that gradually helps us to grow and develop. For others, an intimate relationship may be very healing. For some, a spirituality program or the practice of a spiritual discipline may help to integrate the self and make it whole. For others, a supportive group or a religious community may provide the kind of acceptance and love that lets us become more of who we feel we are meant to be. For some of us, experiences of God's love and caring, in whatever ways these experiences come to us, may be the thing that breaks into the adolescing self, allowing that self to be transformed and to become more adult.

2. *Recovery programs, self-help groups, and counseling and psychotherapy.* If we are suffering from one or more addictions or dependencies, we may find support and direction in recovery programs and in different self-help groups. Recovery programs and groups such as Alcoholics Anonymous (AA) or Narcotics Anonymous (NA) may give us the opportunity to address what is happening in our lives and in our relationships. Besides supporting our efforts to fight the addiction and the dependency, sometimes these programs offer us the opportunity to pay attention to the actual needs of the body-self, to become aware of what we are feeling, to touch some things in the depth, to find our boundaries, to relate in intimacy, and to move toward becoming our own responsible process. Recovery programs and self-help groups may eventually help us become actualizing and reflecting adult selves.

If we are suffering from what others may think of us, we may find in the presence of a counselor or psychotherapist who is concerned for us a safe enough space in which to discover our body-self and what it is feeling, our desires and boundaries, our needs for intimacy, and how we can become our own responsible process. In the presence of a caring other, we may find the freedom and the challenge we need to become an adult self, a self more actualizing and more reflecting.

For some of us, it is through recovery programs, self-help groups, counseling, and psychotherapy—places where the pain and the struggle can be touched and worked with—that we find the love, nurture, respect, and affirmation we are looking for. For some of us, it is in these caring and supportive environments that the contradictions of the Superego God begin to become clearer. For some of us, it is in these caring and supportive environments that the God as Thou, the God of Love, the God of Mystery, the God of Freedom, and the God of Community first appears.

3. Some experiences of suffering, trauma, and loss. Some of us, in experiencing suffering, trauma, and loss, may find a safe and compassionate space in which to begin to accept what happened. In time, we may come to terms with the suffering, the trauma, and the loss, not minimizing what happened but allowing it to become part of a renegotiated and, perhaps, more inclusive sense of self. There is no calculus for suffering, trauma, and loss. Viktor Frankl speaks of the "tragic triad" of suffering, guilt, and death as being at the heart of human experience, calling us to face ourselves and to search for personal meaning in ways that nothing else can.[1] Suffering, trauma, and loss are a two-edged sword for us. At times they make adulthood much harder to realize, and at times they help to usher it in.[2]

4. Challenging societal and cultural constraints, including racism, classism, ageism, and sexism. Since powerful forces in the culture—and sometimes in organized religion—call for conformity to stereotypes around race, class, age, and sex, and since these stereotypes can have such an adverse effect on personal development, often we need to challenge these stereotypes in order to realize adulthood. Because the adult self is an integral self-in-mutuality, this challenge is really twofold. First, we have to challenge the way prejudice lives in us and in the groups we belong to. Then, we have to challenge the way those who are made to be "other" in the society are treated. We need to stand with those discriminated against because of disability, racial and ethnic status, class, age, gender, and sexual orientation. The development of the self and the development of the "other" can only go hand in hand. The truth is that if we cannot uphold the value and dignity of the "other" person, we cannot uphold our own value and dignity.

5. Renegotiating life choices and the repentance of sin. Renegotiating life choices may seem at times like a nearly impossible task. Often we are afraid even to look at the situation we are in that needs to change. We may be convinced that change is out of the question, that nothing could change. We may be convinced that we do not deserve anything to change. We may be convinced that the change would be too difficult, or too unfair, or too confusing, or too late. Often, however, what seems like an impossible situation can, in time, become less impossible when attention is paid to it. Spirituality programs, self-help groups, and counseling and psychotherapy, especially over time, may be helpful in bringing about a new scenario, a way of beginning to live the situation differently, a way of becoming more of an integral self-in-mutuality.

Repentance of sin, as Andras Angyal describes it, is very similar to the process of what often happens in counseling and psychotherapy:

> The act of repentance implies several factors: first, it implies a recognition that one's conduct in some particulars, or one's entire way of life, is unsound; second, it implies an assumption of responsibility for that conduct; third, it implies a sincere regret. All this culminates in the recognition of a complete bankruptcy of one's unwholesome way of life. This then leads to a feeling of humility.[3]

Sometimes what we need to continue becoming an adult self is the humility that comes with repentance, a repentance that includes recognizing what we have done to hinder the self, taking responsibility for what we have done, genuinely regretting what we have done, and then taking steps to change how we are acting. And for Angyal, all of this is only possible with the acceptance, the mutuality, and the caring presence of others or of God.

THINGS THAT FACILITATE RELIGIOUS EXPERIENCING

It seems that whatever puts us in touch with our actual experience of God is helpful in transforming our fettered imaging of God into the unfettered imaging of religious experiencing. In particular, what seems helpful in transforming our fettered imaging of God is to *pay attention* to this imaging just as it presently is—but in light of the adult self that we are or, at least, that we are on the way to becoming. In other words, it is helpful to pay attention to just how we presently are in becoming an integral self-in-mutuality with God and to pay attention to our feeling in relation to God. It is helpful to be open to how we may find God in our depth and how we are presently in our boundaries and in our intimacy with God. Finally, it is helpful to pay attention to the sense of God that emerges from just how we are presently as our own responsible process.

There are any number of ways of paying attention to our present imaging of God so that it can be gradually transformed, even as we are gradually transformed. Nine such ways of paying attention are mentioned briefly here:

1. Praying. Prayer is paying attention to "the self and God together." Prayer is the essence of religion, and it tends, over time, to reveal religious experiencing and the mutual indwelling of the self and the Living God. It is easy, however, to have a rather dichotomized understanding of prayer, which, at least for some of us, makes praying problematic. On the one hand, we may pray to God to intervene in something we care a lot about. We ask God to avert a disaster, to find someone who will bring us happiness, to keep our children safe, to let a loved one get better, to help us be better, to find a good job, to give us peace of mind.

On the other hand, we may pray even though we are not convinced that God intervenes at all. We pray, not because we believe it changes God, but because we find that it changes us. We pray because we find that praying makes us more centered, more accepting, more serene, more loving—in a word, more adult. But praying need not be seen as an "either/or" activity. Rather, praying is paradoxical.[4] It can be understood as a "both/and" activity, an exercise of the self-in-mutuality with God. Praying is paying attention to "the self and God together." Transformation is of "the self and God together" in the direction of mutual openness and availability. It seems that reality changes as God becomes more real.

One of the traditional definitions of prayer is "the lifting of the heart and mind to God." A kind of praying that is, perhaps, most transformative of ourselves, of our world, and of our relationship with God is the kind of praying that comes as much as possible from the body-self (with the "heart" and the "mind" together), the kind of praying that comes from our feeling and from our depth, the kind of praying that honors our present boundaries and our present relationship with God, the kind of praying that comes from our own responsible process, just as we presently have it. Sometimes this kind of praying helps us experience a God as Thou or Spiritual Presence, a God of Love, a God of Mystery, a God of Freedom, and a God of Community.

2. *Sharing faith.* Sometimes sharing our faith and hearing others share their faith becomes a genuine dialogue in which the body-self, the feeling, the depth, the boundaries, the intimacy, and the sense of responsibility of each person is touched and moved in a way that helps to transform fettered imaging of God. Sharing faith can be extremely powerful in moving us closer to the unfettered imaging of religious experiencing, especially when it is done in an atmosphere in which mutuality is honored and each person's experience is respected. In such an atmosphere, the God as Thou, the God of Love, the God of Mystery, the God of Freedom, and the God of Community can be wonderfully revealed, even as we experience ourselves as more and more an integral self-in-mutuality.

3. *Worship services.* Sometimes in attending worship services, our relationship with God is experienced in the body-self, in feeling, and in the depth. Sometimes these worship services honor and celebrate our boundaries; sometimes they draw us into intimacy with God; sometimes they affirm us as our own responsibility before God. We leave the worship service feeling strengthened in our efforts to be responsible adults and feeling once more the presence and empowerment of the Living God. We have been with the God as Thou or the Spiritual Presence. We have been welcomed by the God of Love, we have sensed the God of Mystery, we have experienced the God of Freedom, and we have been enveloped in the God of Community. Sometimes worship services are wonderfully helpful in facilitating our religious experiencing.

Sometimes, however, worship services are not helpful at all in facilitating our religious experiencing. Sometimes worship services are purely in the service of keeping adolescing selves under the control of the Superego God. Perhaps such services are conducted by the religious leaders in a way that reinforces authoritarianism, rationalism, and anthropomorphism within the group. Perhaps the only God worshipped in these services is the Supreme Being, the God of Law, the God of Belief, the God of Dependency and Control, and the God of the Group. Perhaps we leave the worship service no more adult than when we came. The ritual power of worship services can be very strong, but unfortunately that power can be in the service of control as well as in the service of transformation.

4. Meditation. Any form of meditation that centers us in the body-self, in our feeling, and in our depth, any form of meditation that helps us with our boundaries and our sense of the other, any form of meditation that lets us be more our own responsible process, can bring us closer to our sense of ourselves and therefore closer to an unfettered imaging of God.[5] Often meditation is understood as a form of reflective prayer that focuses on various religious themes or topics. To the extent that this kind of meditation lets us pay attention to "the self and God together," it may also further our religious experiencing.

Thomas Merton's understanding of meditation is helpful. "Reflection involves not only the mind but also the heart, and indeed our whole being. One who really meditates does not merely think, he also loves, and by his love—or at least by his sympathetic intuition into the reality upon which he reflects—he enters into that reality and knows it so to speak from within, by a kind of identification."[6] This kind of meditation, a meditation of love and empathy, a meditation that engages our "whole being," is directly in the service of religious experiencing.

5. Contemplation. If meditation should turn into contemplation—contemplation being understood as "attending the other in love"—then one way we have of transforming our fettered imaging of God into the unfettered imaging of religious experiencing is, with openness and love, to allow the body-self in its feeling, in its depth, and in its boundaries to "gaze upon," "move toward," "be with," and "rest in" another person, or a group of people, or any reality needing to experience love.

This kind of contemplation not only allows a God as Thou or Spiritual Presence, a God of Love, a God of Mystery, a God of Freedom, and a God of Community to be revealed, but it also allows our sense of self to come into some further sense of wholeness as well.

It is, of course, also possible to contemplate God—even as it is possible to experience God as contemplating us. As a body-self in feeling, in depth, with clear boundaries, in intimacy, and as our own responsible process, we can "gaze upon," "move toward," "be with," and "rest in" God, finding in the process, perhaps, a God as Thou, a God of Love, a God of Mystery, a God of Freedom, and a God of Community.

Often a very powerful experience, contemplation facilitates religious experiencing, even as it is an exercise of the reflecting self-in-mutuality. Its meaning can, however, become hollow and gradually disappear if the love experienced in contemplation does not find some generative expression. What is there for us in contemplation often needs to be affirmed in some way by the actualizing self-in-mutuality. As Thomas Keating puts it, "Contemplative prayer without action stagnates, and action without contemplative prayer leads to burn-out or running around in circles."[7]

6. Art, music, drama, reading, and study. Art and music, especially when they capture paradox and metaphor, can often be directly in the service of religious experiencing. Art and music, in a way that is often quite powerful, can directly evoke religious meaning in the feeling and depth of the body-self. Drama that touches human and religious themes, for example, the wonderful story of *Les Misérables*, can touch the body-self in its feeling and in its depth and challenge an adult experience of God. Reading such texts as sacred scripture, biographies of religious figures, religious essays, and poetry, likewise, can challenge our fettered imaging of God, helping us, perhaps, to let go of some of our fantasy, our relating in transference, and our logic of objective knowing.

Studying, especially in the area of the humanities, the social sciences, and religion, can also challenge our fettered imaging of God, helping to transform that imaging into religious experiencing. If our interest in studying is for transformation as well as for information, often that studying has a way, especially over time, of facilitating adulthood and adult religion together.

7. Pastoral counseling. Some of us may find in pastoral counseling a safe place in which to explore whatever might be hindering the body-self in its feeling and in its depth, a safe place in which to sort out boundary questions and questions of intimacy as we work toward becoming our own responsible process in relation to others and to God.[8] William Hulme defines pastoral counseling as "a ministry to persons, couples, and families that assists them in working through pressing problems in their relationship to themselves, to others, and to God."[9] Pastoral counseling is a practice concerned for "pressing problems" with whomever or in whatever we find ourselves related to.

The uniqueness of pastoral counseling is that it offers us a space where who we are personally and who we are religiously are not dichotomized. In pastoral counseling, our personal experience and our religious experience can be considered together, especially as that experience is confused, conflicted, problematic, or growth inhibiting in some way. In other words, the uniqueness of pastoral counseling lies in the fact that the things that hinder the adult self and the things that hinder adult religion can receive attention and be transformed at the same time. Using slightly different language than we are using here, James Ewing describes the kind of twofold transformation that pastoral counseling is able to bring about:

What we know of psychological personality structure and religious symbols allows us to understand the conflict or stress a person is suffering. If the conflict is resolved through the pastor-therapist's intervention, then change takes place both in the development of healthier personality and of more adequate "God-symbols" (i.e., ideas, and expressions for relating to God) that allow internal meaning and direction to shift. Psychological structures and religious symbols intertwine so that one intimately affects the other.[10]

8. Spiritual mentoring. For some of us—especially the more we are "reasonably coherent" adult selves—the presence of a mentor who is mature in religious experiencing and who lets us explore our own relationship with God can be very helpful in the realization of our own religious experiencing. Such a person—perhaps a trained spiritual director or guide—can provide a safe space in which we can pay attention to the experience of God of the body-self in its feeling and in its depth. With the help of such a person, we can gradually own our boundaries in relation to God, we can explore intimacy with God, and we can become our own responsible process in relation to God.[11] Spiritual mentoring can further our relationship with God, even as it can further the adult self.

Unfortunately, if we are left to our own devices, it is often very hard for us to let our fettered imaging of God become transformed, no matter how hard we try. As we have seen, even if we are adult in the other areas of our lives, the staying power of fantasy, relating in transference, and the logic of objective knowing in our relationship with God is often much too strong for us to overcome on our own. Often, a spiritual mentor—hopefully, a caring and encouraging person, a person of integrity and wisdom—can be extremely helpful, allowing us to find the focus, the clarity, and the support we need. We must be careful, however, not to let the spiritual mentor take us down a road that is not our own. As Sandra Schneiders cautions:

> The only valid objective of spiritual direction is growth of the directee. What growth consists in for the person in question is not to be determined by the guide, much less by a third party. It must be worked out by the directee in his/her relationship with God. The spiritual guide is at the service of the directee's own spiritual project, not of someone else's (or the director's own!) project for the person.[12]

9. Everyday life. Finally, life itself may invite us in any number of ways to pay attention to who we are with our God. A touch, a glance, a surprising kindness, an act of courage, an event in nature, a crisis of some kind, an experience of forgiveness—these are some of the ways that the presence of God can at times evoke the body-self in its feeling and in its depth. These are some of the ways we find our boundaries, we realize intimacy, and we become our own responsible process with our God.

THINGS THAT FACILITATE THE LIVING GOD

What facilitates the transformation of the Superego God into the Living God are, of course, *the experiences we have of a Living God.*

The experiences of a God as Thou or a Spiritual Reality, the experiences of a God of Love, the experiences of a God of Mystery, the experiences of a God of Freedom, and the experiences of a God of Community are ultimately what allow for the transformation of the Superego God. In addition, these experiences—perhaps over time—may facilitate the transformation of an adolescing self into an adult self because, in these experiences, we tend to find ourselves loved and accepted by God in a way that lets us change and grow. And these experiences—perhaps over time—may also facilitate the transformation of fettered imaging into the unfettered imaging of religious experiencing because, in these experiences, fantasy, relating in transference, and the logic of objective knowing are neither operative nor needed.

Experiences of the Living God—experiences often as unique as they are powerful—can come to us at any time in our lives, even when we are very young. It seems that we do not control when and how the Living God becomes present to us. The closer we are, however, to becoming adult selves with unfettered imaging, the more whatever experiences of the Living God we might have can be part of adult religion, that is, the more these experiences are part of our ongoing religious experiencing, part of our sense of ourselves together with God.

Of all the different ways the Superego God may be transformed by the Living God, there are three overall stances we can try to develop—the closer we are to functioning as adult selves—that may facilitate this transformation.

1. Surrendering control. If needing to control God to get what we want in life is an overall reason why we hold on to the Superego God, even if we are functioning as an adult self, then surrendering control is a stance we can practice—often in the face of suffering, guilt, and death—that may welcome the Living God. Surrendering control over what can happen in life may provide the space and the opportunity for the God as Thou, the God of Love, the God of Mystery, the God of Freedom, and the God of Community to be with us. Surrendering control cannot be forced, but—especially with the help of ritual—it can often be allowed. When we surrender control over what happens to us in life, we touch something beyond warrant in the depth of our humanness, and we touch something beyond warrant in mystery as well. Surrendering control is often very transformative. It may be the very thing that eventually lets us claim the self as an integral self-in-mutuality, even as it opens us up to the possibility of experiencing the Living God.

2. *Welcoming hope and forgiveness.* If needing to hold God accountable is an overall reason why we hold on to the Superego God, even if we are functioning as an adult self, then welcoming hope and forgiveness is a stance we can practice—often in the face of suffering, guilt, and death—that may provide the space and the opportunity for the Living God to be with us. Hope and forgiveness cannot be forced, but—especially with the help of ritual—they can often be allowed. When we hope and when we forgive, we deny neither the reality nor the effects of evil. Rather, we hold for a further and a deeper reality in which, as William James phrases it, "natural evil is swallowed up in supernatural good."[13] When we hope and when we forgive, we touch something beyond warrant in the depth of our humanness, and we touch something beyond warrant in mystery as well. Welcoming hope and forgiveness is often very transformative. As our response to evil, it may be the very thing that eventually lets us reclaim the self as an integral self-in-mutuality, even as it opens us up to the possibility of experiencing the Living God.

3. *Engaging in an integral spirituality.* Another way of allowing the Superego God to be transformed is to find and actively pursue a spirituality that engages who we are as actualizing and reflecting selves. In the different ways we "go out to the other," for example, in a mutuality of care and justice, and in the different ways we "come home to ourselves," for example, in different practices that allow for reflection and meditation, we may provide the space and the opportunity for the God as Thou, the God of Love, the God of Mystery, the God of Freedom, and the God of Community to be with us. When we engage in what is for us an integral spirituality, we often touch something in the depth of our humanness, and we often touch something in mystery as well. Engaging in an integral spiritually is often very transformative. It may be the very thing that eventually lets us fully be

an integral self-in-mutuality, even as it opens us up to the possibility of experiencing the Living God.

Finally, if it is quite true, as we have seen, that organized religion can hinder our experience of the Living God, it is also quite true that organized religion can facilitate our experiencing of that God. Three characteristics of organized religion that can facilitate the transformation of the Superego God into the Living God are mentioned here.

Mutuality

An organized religion that fosters mutuality makes real dialogue and true community possible among its members. Mutuality, as Erik Erikson suggests, means that what one person needs to receive, another person is able to give, and what one person is able to give, another person is able to receive.[14] Mutuality means that the body-self of some of us, in its feeling and in its depth, can be available to the body-self of others of us, in its feeling and in its depth. Mutuality means that there is an "equivalence between persons, a concomitant valuing of each other, a common regard marked by trust, respect, and affection."[15] Mutuality means that justice and care for each person within the community is essential and that justice and care for each person in the broader world community and for the environment within which we live is equally essential.

Mutuality helps to transform authoritarianism, rationalism, and anthropomorphism in organized religion. In a religion of mutuality, leadership surfaces from within the community itself. In a religion of mutuality, freedom and responsibility are valued over control. In a religion of mutuality, unity and diversity are valued over conformity. In a religion of mutuality, each person's understanding of God is honored and respected. In a religion of mutuality, adults are able to share openly with other adults, and the voice of the Living God can be heard.

Concern for mutuality in organized religion provides the space and the opportunity for "the self and God together" to develop in the individual and in the community. The adult self is honored and furthered when mutuality is honored and respected. Religious experiencing finds nourishment in mutuality. In real, interpersonal understanding and support, the reality of Living God can be discovered. Quite simply, paying attention to mutuality in organized religion facilitates the revelation of the Living God. A God as Thou, a God of Love, a God of Mystery, a God of Freedom, and a God of Community is at home in organized religion when mutuality is respected.

Experience

An organized religion that honors the experience of all its members makes for real dialogue and true community. Experience that is respected and can be shared enriches everyone. What touches one or more of us as a body-self with feeling and depth is able to touch others of us as a body-self with feeling and depth. Real listening and real dialogue are possible on the basis of respect for experience. Real understanding and real support—the basis of any community—are possible on the basis of respect for each person's experience.

Respect for the experience of each person helps to transform authoritarianism, rationalism, and anthropomorphism in organized religion. In a religion of experience, the imaging of God that each person brings is vital. In a religion of experience, our actual relationship with God is valued over beliefs and objective facts about God. In a religion of experience, the body-self in its feeling and in its depth in relation with God is valued over reason and over concepts about God that come from "the mind." In a religion of experience, our relating with God can easily be in dialogue with the events of our lives. In a religion of experience, adults are able to share openly with other adults, and the voice of the Living God can be heard.

Concern for experience in organized religion provides the space and the opportunity for "the self and God together" to develop in the individual and in the community. The adult self is honored and furthered as it respects its own experience and is challenged by the experience of others. Religious experiencing finds nourishment in experience. In getting as close as possible to our actual experiences of God, the reality of God can be discovered. Quite simply, paying attention to experience in organized religion facilitates the revelation of the Living God. A God as Thou, a God of Love, a God of Mystery, a God of Freedom, and a God of Community is at home in organized religion when experience is respected.

Mystery

Finally, an organized religion that allows for mystery makes for real dialogue and true community among its members. "Mystery," as Parker Palmer observes, "surrounds every deep experience of the human heart: the deeper we go into the heart's darkness or light, the closer we get to the ultimate mystery of God."[16] Mystery provides a safe, symbolic space for new and fuller meaning to emerge in each one of us and in the community as a whole. Mystery provides a safe, symbolic space for change and growth in each one of us and in the community as a whole. Mystery provides a safe, symbolic space for the paradox that holds us together in tension and that lets us move forward together. In mystery, the body-self of each us, in its feeling and in its depth, is connected to the Living God.

Mystery helps to transform authoritarianism, rationalism, and anthropomorphism in organized religion. In a religion of mystery, depth is valued over conventionality. In a religion of mystery, rituals that are able to touch the body-self in its feeling and its depth are valued over beliefs and verbal formulations. In a religion of mystery, metaphor is valued over literal thinking. In a religion of mystery, reality lives in paradox rather than in dichotomies. In a religion of mystery, meaning is valued over propositional truth. In a religion of mystery, adults are able to share openly with other adults, and the voice of the Living God can be heard.

Concern for mystery in organized religion provides the space and the opportunity for "the self and God together" to develop in the individual and in the community. The adult self is honored and furthered when mystery is respected. Religious experiencing finds nourishment in mystery. In the depth allowed for in mystery, the reality of God can be discovered. The possibility for surrendering control lies within mystery. The possibility of welcoming hope and forgiveness lies within mystery. Quite simply, paying attention to mystery in organized religion facilitates the revelation of the Living God. A God as Thou, a God of Love, a God of Freedom, a God of Community, and, of course, a God of Mystery is at home in organized religion when mystery is respected.

NOTES

1. See Viktor E. Frankl, "The Philosophical Foundations of Logotherapy," in *Psychotherapy and Existentialism* (New York: Washington Square Press, 1967), 29.

2. See Robert Grant, *The Way of the Wound: A Spirituality of Trauma and Transformation* (Oakland, CA: Robert Grant, 1996). See also Deborah A. Barrett, "Suffering and the Process of Transformation," *The Journal of Pastoral Care* 53, no. 4 (Winter 1999): 461–72.

3. Andras Angyal, "The Convergence of Psychotherapy and Religion," *The Journal of Pastoral Care* 5, no. 4 (1951): 9–10.

4. See Bernard Tickerhoof, *Paradox: The Spiritual Path to Transformation* (Mystic, CT: Twenty-third Publications, 2002).

5. For a good introduction to meditation, see Lawrence LeShan, *How to Meditate: A Guide to Self-Discovery* (New York: Bantam, 1974).

6. Thomas Merton, *Spiritual Direction and Meditation* (Collegeville, MN: The Liturgical Press, 1960), 52.

7. Thomas Keating, *Intimacy with God* (New York: Crossroad, 1994), 159.

8. See John J. Shea, "Adult Faith, Pastoral Counseling, and Spiritual Direction," *The Journal of Pastoral Care* 51, no. 3 (Fall 1997): 259–70.

9. William E. Hulme, *Pastoral Care and Counseling: Using the Unique Resources of the Christian Tradition* (Minneapolis, MN: Augsburg, 1981), 9.

10. James W. Ewing, "The Pastoral Therapeutic Stance," in *Psychiatry, Ministry and Pastoral Counseling*, ed. A. W. Richard Sipe and Clarence J. Rowe (Collegeville, MN: The Liturgical Press, 1984), 66.

11. See Ewing, "The Pastoral Therapeutic Stance." See also Joann W. Conn, *Spirituality and Personal Maturity* (New York: Paulist Press, 1989).

12. Sandra M. Schneiders, "The Contemporary Ministry of Spiritual Direction," *Chicago Studies* 15 (Spring 1976): 126.

13. William James, *The Varieties of Religious Experience* (Cambridge, MA: Harvard University Press, 1985), 131.

14. See Erik H. Erikson, "Eight Ages of Man," in *Childhood and Society*, 2nd rev. and enl. ed. (New York: Norton, 1963).

15. Elizabeth A. Johnson, *She Who Is: The Mystery of God in Feminist Discourse* (New York: Crossroad, 1992), 68.

16. Parker Palmer, *Let Your Life Speak: Listening for the Voice of Vocation* (San Francisco: Jossey-Bass, 2000), 60.

14

IMAGES OF
TRANSFORMATION

This chapter on images of transformation comes from stories of
chronological adults whose imaging of God is being transformed in some way. Some of the storytellers are in recovery from
alcohol or drugs. Some are in counseling or psychotherapy. Others
are in some form of spiritual mentoring. The stories themselves are,
for the most part, interchangeable with the stories of the Living
God, no doubt because all experiences of the Living God are transformative in some way. What is especially pronounced in these stories are the honesty, the humility, and the courage of the different
storytellers. These are stories of pain and suffering, but they are
stories not so much of being broken but of being broken open. In
these stories, "the journey into self is the journey into God, and the
journey into God is the journey into self."

In these stories, the transformation is of "the self and God together." As the struggle for authenticity and responsibility becomes
real in the storyteller, the Living God becomes real, and as the Living
God become real, the struggle of authenticity and responsibility becomes real. What can be seen in these stories is that as the self becomes more and more its own body-self, in its feeling, in its depth, in
its clear boundaries, in its need for intimacy, and in its taking of responsibility, God becomes more and more a God as Thou, a God of
Love, a God of Mystery, a God of Freedom, and a God of Community.

IMAGES OF GOD

Peter

Peter is a man in his forties, divorced, and with two teenage children. He is in Alcoholics Anonymous (AA). He has been sober now for several years. When we started the interview, he was not quite sure whether or not he had anything to say. He just wanted to be honest. For years, it seems, he lived with a sense of himself that came from how others saw him and from how he thought he should present himself. All of that was beginning to change, and he wanted to say as carefully as he could what was happening, as if he were savoring the things he was finding in himself.

Since I've been in the AA program, my image of God has been changing. What I perceived God to be previously is not necessarily what He is. I think I'm coming to a belief that I can't separate God from life. I used to separate God from my life and from what was going on around me. God was up there somewhere in the heavens, and now God and life are one and the same thing. I've only started to think about these things since I've been in the program actively. I'm still growing in this. God and life are together. God is in me, and I am in God. And the same for you. We are in the image and likeness of God, and his presence is right here all the time—not off somewhere in heaven. This is new for me, because before I never felt the need to delve into these things. I realize now that my life isn't going so well, and hopefully I'm trying to do something about that.

Up until very recently, my understanding of God was all wrapped up in religious belief or religious tradition that was taught to me. I was told that I was to believe this, that, or the other thing. Everything I believed I was taught through the church. I guess one thing I have found is that I can have, and I can be comfortable with, my own personal relation with God. That my relationship doesn't have to be the same as yours. My beliefs can be different, my attitudes can be different. And that creates a very comfortable situation in my mind, at least, that I don't have to feel guilt over not necessarily accepting everything that the church taught or, at least, what I thought the church taught.

I have come to understand that I am human, I am weak, I have de-fects, and that God loves me as much as anyone else. I have much less guilt now, not an excuse for what I may have done, but a better un-derstanding, perhaps, of why I commit sin. There was a lot of inter-nal turmoil and guilt. I was less than good, less than perfect, not as good as I could be, and I really beat myself up, taking myself much too seriously. I had to present the image that I was perfect, that I was a certain way, but internally knowing I was far different. I was a crowd pleaser, a people pleaser, trying to be what I thought other people wanted, and what I thought I was.

When I was growing up, I would get all sorts of compliments from the parents of my friends. Even teachers would single me out and say, "Why can't you be more like Peter? He's such a nice young man." I liked to hear that in a way because it built up my self-esteem, but all the time, I didn't feel part of things. I felt sort of alone and sort of isolated. But I accepted what people were saying as who I was, and therefore, I had to be that. In those days, I didn't give much thought to God, but I practiced my re-ligious faith because that was being good and because that was being what God wanted of me, but I never went beyond that, perhaps for most of my life.

I've been in the AA program for several years now, and I found it was a spiritual program, a place where I could come and be comfortable. The other people in the program were the same as me. They had the same feel-ings, even though the individual experiences may have been different. They had the same fear, and anger, and anxiety, and questions of self-esteem—any number of characteristics we seemed to have in common. This is the first place I have heard people sharing their inner lives, their feelings, the things that they had done. I have shared the things that I may have done, that I always had guilt about. Being part of AA may not have increased my religion, but it has made me more spiritual. I'm grow-ing in the way Christ intended us to live. There's a feeling of spiritual-ity. I understand that I am a good person, that God understands me and loves me despite my slips. And I judge other people less.

For me, spirituality is an inner contact with God. There's an inner feeling of peace that I may have, contentment, and acceptance of my situation. There's a trust there. For me, these things are God working within me. I have to be concerned for what I'm doing, for what God expects of me. I think about God more often, and I try to do something nice for someone else, to reach out to someone else whenever I can during the day. The feeling I have now is that I am responsible. That's what I get from the program: "I am responsible." Part of going to meetings is to be there for other people. God is there when I take responsibility for other people as well as for myself. I experience the Higher Power through the rooms of AA.

Lisa

Lisa is a married woman with adult children who is also in AA. When she was a child, her parents sent her to church. They were raised in two different Christian denominations and were not interested in religion that much, but they thought that Lisa should attend church on Sundays. She used to like going to church, but eventually her parents did not go to church at all. She would come home from church and ask her parents questions. The things said there about God were confusing to her, and sometimes even terrifying, leaving her with a lot of uncertainty about the teachings of religion. When I asked her how she imaged God, she immediately said,

I have problems with the pictures up here in my head. I've always been searching for what God is because of the garbage I got when I was a kid. Like if I start thinking about God, I'm afraid. It's gotta come from my heart. I don't see anything. I feel God. There is some kind of force. It's nonjudgmental, loving, and it can be accessed. It's inside me. I know it sounds very trite, but "God is love" makes sense to me. The picture of the guy with the beard on the cloud never did.

I asked Lisa if she ever had an experience of God, and she started to talk about a very difficult time in her life. Then she became silent and began to choke up. When she was able to continue, she said:

I had just started a Course in Miracles, and my journey was depression and anxiety. I had a great deal of depression, but I wasn't hospitalized. I would go to therapy, and I was searching because I was in pain. And this one morning, I woke up, and I said, "I am so depressed."

And there was a voice, it was like an inner voice, like a communication. And it said, "Why are you depressed?" And I said, "I'm depressed because I'm angry." The voice said, "What are you so angry about"? And I said, "I'm angry about this and this and this." And the voice said, "It's okay to remain angry about all those things, but just remember they are neither right or wrong. They just are." And then the voice said, "I will never, never, never, never leave you alone." And I have to tell you that I was at peace for days. It totally lifted that depressed feeling. Oh, man! It's like a lot of strength, very knowing, very loving. I could cry thinking about this.

I don't control much of anything since my sobriety. I get into trouble when I think I do. That's why AA is a relief. AA is a relief because you get the first step, "I am powerless over alcohol." You come to believe that a power greater than yourself can restore you to sanity. And then you let that happen. And what a relief. Because a lot of people come into AA saying, "Oh, I can do this on my own," and they go through hell. What happens in the steps is that you start to clean house, and you start to look at what your part is in your relationships. Everybody has a story. It's not just the drinking. For a lot of us, drinking is a symptom. Plus, there are some of us who I believe have the disease of alcoholism.

For me, it started with my husband. Mainly we had a relationship in which he was the dominant one, and I was always the one to protect him. So I accepted it. I tried to do everything right, and everything right meant that whatever this man wanted was right. And if I couldn't do it right, in my case I ended up drinking in order to try to continue to be this person. And then, when I couldn't do that anymore, that was the beginning of a whole new life for me, because then I became much more of an individual. There have been a lot of conflicts, but life has gotten even better as a result of all of this.

I was slowly getting hooked on alcohol. I would ask people, "Do you think I have a problem?" And they would say, "Oh no, not you, you're fine." But I was sneaky about it. I was drinking in the morning, every morning in the morning. I was doing that for a couple of months. And one morning, I stood up, and in the middle of my kitchen, I just started to cry. And I said, "Oh, what's happening to me?" And I just walked

*over to the phone, picked up the phone, and looked at it. I knew nothing.
When I was younger, I thought AA was a bunch of crazy cultists. I
called, and what I experienced was pure love. They said, "Okay, we'll
get you to a meeting." I found this meeting, and I knew—it was the next
meeting—that I had to get there. I was searching and searching and finally God grabbed me by the back of the head and said, "Okay, lady,
you've got to clean up this act or you're never going to get it."*

*So what do I find in these rooms today? I find unconditional love for
the most part. People do not judge you. All of a sudden, I'm telling these
things about myself, and instead of shame and instead of anger at anybody, they accept you. I can say who I am. My responsibility is to be honest with myself, to see the God in other people, and to see the God in me.
In AA, they talk about the God of your understanding. A lot of people
just say it's the wounds of AA, it's the people of the fellowship. I think it's
bigger than that. For me, it's the force that's there all the time. It's also
where I remember the connections, that we are all equal, that there is a
call to love. When I don't see it's a call to love, I experience myself as a
victim. I forget God. That's how prayer works. I remember my connection with God.*

*Without the spirituality, you don't get well. I experience it in AA. I
think you could have your whole spirituality in AA. I also experience it
in the Course in Miracles. After a while, I'm aware that the truth you
can find all over the place, that we are all born loving and whole and
connected. I have always been searching for what really is the truth and
for what really is important. Today, I do not have a desire to join a
church. With all the stuff I do, it would be overload. I need to have some
time. But I feel differently when the holidays come. I look at them from
afar. I find my religion in the rooms of AA—my connection and my re-
membering of God—and in the Course in Miracles.*

Alice

Alice is the "scaredy cat as a kid" whom we met in chapter 5. She is a
social worker on the staff of a community agency, often seeing children
who have been abused. Alice recalled a time in her mid-twenties, a
time that was a turning point in her imaging of God.

I think the bottom fell out back then. I was kind of clueless, not know-ing. I mean I had a job, I had all the externals, but I had nothing in-ternally. There was nothing there. It absolutely felt like nothingness, like there was nothing there, nothing to wake up for the next day, just nothing. It was a scary place to be. But maybe that is where God really can get to you. At least, that's the way I see it. I think it's when you re-ally, you know, are at the end of your rope that . . . well, it's hard to ex-plain. Anyway, He spoke to me like you read in books. He said, "I'm here." It probably sounds like I had some kind of a verbal apparition or something, which it wasn't. It was just a sense, a strong sense, of "Come on out."

Nobody, nobody, no priest, no parental figure came to me and said, "You need God now. Come and go to church every Sunday." Something inside just told me that's where to go. I used to see the ad from the church every Christmas and Easter. It would say, "Come home for Christmas," "Come home for Easter." And that would . . . that would kind of tug at me, you know. So looking back at it, I can say that it was a process that was probably always there, but I just wasn't aware of as strongly until I turned twenty-six. Although I can look at times when I think I was be-ing called back, and a few other times that I tried to go back, and noth-ing would happen, for whatever reason. And I've fallen a million times since, and I've been confused a million times since, but He still forgave me. He still said, "You can come back." Which makes me think He must be very loving and incredibly patient. There's a more consistent sense of God there. It grows.

Toward the end of our conversation, Alice shared an experience of God that was very powerful for her, one that has a lot to do with her sense of God's presence.

This is true, this is really true. And I was sober as a judge. It was two o'clock in the afternoon. I felt terrible that day, you know, like really a horrible person—I'm kind of embarrassed even to talk about this, but what the heck. My mom had a painting that I didn't even really like so much, but I always would ask her so many times, so she painted this painting. So, this one day, I came home, and I was trying to say the rosary every day. So, I go, okay, now it'll be a good thing to do, sit down on my couch—and this is the truth. I was just sitting on the couch, my mom's painting was across from me, and I was just saying the rosary, feeling like, you know, you're probably a hypocrite even doing this.

And then, just this feeling. I mean it actually—it's never happened since, it's never happened before. Somebody was there. That's how real it felt. And it felt scary, and I didn't know what to do. I just kept praying and saying, "What the heck is this? I don't know what this is." And then it wasn't scary anymore—it was just like this is something. I don't know what it is, but it's something. It felt . . . it felt like I was surrounded by something. I mean, I know this sounds . . . dumb, crazy. It was like, I mean it was . . . I was so grateful for it, you know.

And then I said, "If I look at that painting, it's gonna turn into something." That was it. And I looked. And so help me God, it changed. It did. And I know it sounds berserk, like they should bring me up to, you know, the state hospital or something. But it started to change. And then I got even more scared. I was scared enough with this physical kind of sense being on, and then the picture started changing, and I go, "Oh man! What is this?" And I don't know. So, do I just keep saying the rosary? At least then I can focus on something. But I couldn't stop watching it. And it started to change. Like this color, like this orange-like color kept moving, like, just kind of spreading out from the corner.

And then I could see an eye, something like an eye. And I thought, "Oh my God, what is this?" And the whole time it was like, "Yeah, I'm watching it, but what is this craziness?" And then I could see another eye, but it was too far away to look like a face, you know. It was too . . . too not proportional enough for it to be a face. The eyes were too far apart. And different, they were different. One was more like a profile eye, and one was like more an eye looking right at you. And I can remember it like it was yesterday. And the orange color just kept coming out, and then, you know, from pictures that I've seen of Our Lord, it was what looked like to be His face, but, like, from a profile. And it's the weirdest thing. Nothing else changed in it.

You know, I was hoping it would say, "This is what you're supposed to do." I was hoping it was going to be like a direct statement, like, "Do this with your life." Nothing like that. I can remember that feeling, whatever that feeling was, leaving and then looking and thinking, "Now what am I supposed to do after this?" You know, it's funny now, but the whole rest of the day I kept saying, "That was crazy," and "You must be crazy," and "Am I getting too religious or whatever?" But to this day, I'll kind of look, and I can still see it. But I know I'm not crazy. And I look, and I can still see it, and it makes me feel peaceful. It's like some kind of personal sign, like the presence of God, and I can still kind of feel it. Who knows? Maybe I won't ever know. Maybe it's just something that you can only appreciate for yourself, and no one else will. It just feels good to me that it happened, and that's enough.

I asked Alice what her relationship with God was like for her now.

Now it does feel more like a relationship. Like He knows me already, you know, like there's nothing you can hide from Him. There's nothing He doesn't know about you already, and still, still He loves you, you know. And He's patient. And that just feels a lot healthier to me now than it did even two years ago, before I went into spiritual direction. I've kind of lessened my performance stance towards God a little bit. And I don't have to be responsible for God, just my response, just how I respond and how I choose to live my life. I believe this, that a person has a potential that He's given us, and that He does want to see us realize that. I used to think I was gonna get some message about what to do. Now I'm realizing that you've got to make some choices. And if they're wrong choices, you're gonna know. He's gonna let you know.

Whatever transformation has happened—and I've been in some scary places since then—it feels different. Like I see it now as something in process. I see some terrible things in my work. Just last week there was this little kid who was burned on most of his body by his own mother. And people say, "Why is this happening? Why does God allow this to happen?" I admit to them that I don't know. I don't feel that I have to explain everything to everyone anymore. It's been a relief. I'm a social worker in this place, and I try to be a good Christian. I don't know what the ultimate answers are. Maybe parts of me are back in the fifth grade or whatever. I don't know. It's in process. Every day I just try to do what I can.

Elizabeth

Elizabeth is another woman we met earlier in chapter 5. She had a "rules relationship with God" and suffered with "problems of scrupulosity" for many years. In midlife, she had a long and challenging ordeal with a very serious form of cancer. In that whole experience, and in her struggle to find herself, she experienced a great deal of transformation, in herself and in her relationship with God.

Getting cancer, that was the crisis. Actually, I have had cancer twice. The first time was about eight years ago, and I just tried to hide it. You know, "I'm gonna get over this, and I'm not gonna die." It was that kind of thing, and then I got better. The second time it was more serious. They sent me home to die. Later, when another doctor finally decided to operate on me, I was in the hospital almost six weeks. The first time, I think I was just angry. The second time was a different realization, a completely different realization. It brought me to an aloneness, a complete and utter aloneness—it's hard for me to talk about it. I knew that everything on this earth is kind of like nothing. And it felt like there wasn't anybody there for me. There was no person—except the people in the hospital—that was really there for me. When you realize that you're stripped of almost everything, then you begin to hope that there's something bigger for you. That was the crisis.

At first, I was ready to die. I don't think that I was ready in that I had lived, you know. It was very sad. It was sad because I had never lived, spiritually. But I was ready to accept that I had to die. It was like I gave up or something. It was like, "Well, this is it. I'm gonna go through this, and then I'm gonna die." But it was dreaming from my childhood, like a cult thing. When I was in grade school, we were given this vision of a happy death, and I remember thinking as a child, "Well, wouldn't it be nice to die of cancer, lying in bed, absolved from all your sins, completely forgiven by God, just lying there waiting to die." And that's exactly what happened to me. It's very sad. To be like that, to be taught all that as a child. Those children are taught like that with all that fear.

After they sent me home to die, I found another doctor—the doctor who eventually operated on me—and I got into therapy. This therapist taught me to go inside my body and to actually envision the doctor cutting my stomach open and opening the cells up. She was hypnotizing me, but I was not fully under. She allowed me to accept the operation and not be so scared of it. I got through the operation fine. She helped me to find a trusting kind of openness. I learned to go with my body, to trust my instincts in my body. It wasn't enough spiritually. I didn't really understand that part yet. But while I was going to her for help, I realized there was a lot of other things, you know, like there was a lot of anger inside of me, there was a lot of resentment, there was a lot of other issues that I hadn't come to terms with. So, therapy with her was very helpful, but mostly physically and mentally rather than spiritually. I learned a lot about my own internal powers, so that kind of calmed me. But that wasn't enough. That wasn't going to the core.

Then, when I went thorough the operation and all the recovery in the hospital, I thought that I had been purged spiritually. I thought that it didn't matter that I didn't have my own basis for religion. And then, you know, I wasn't scrupulous, and I wasn't worried about the rules. There were more important things to think about. But it wasn't true. The experience in the hospital was very healing, and a number of really beautiful things happened to me there, between the doctors and me and different members of the staff. But it still didn't relieve me of the scrupulosity or any of that. As soon as I started to heal physically, then those old feelings started coming back. It was like when I was free to die, then I was free to be, but just for a little while. And that's when I knew that I needed to be healed spiritually. If I wasn't going to die right away, then I had better figure out how to live.

The difference is therapy. When I went through therapy the second time, everything in the room changed. I was dealing with all those things I could never let myself feel. I was angry at myself for what I did to myself all those years, angry that I wasn't empowered enough to be able to change, or speak up, or be personally responsible. Therapy was a kind of empowerment, I'd say, a personal empowerment for myself. And that affected my religion, because if I couldn't be this total person who was empowered, how could I totally empower myself to believe in God? How could I have a close relationship with God, if I wasn't personally empowered myself? So, I think it was more of a change in my personality, and that affected what I believed spiritually.

Personal responsibility, that's the change. Personal empowerment. Not to look to others to guide me, or to tell me what to do, or to show me the way. I sort of knew, I guess, that inside of me there was a personal way or a personal choice for me. And my relationship with God would have to be totally personal and not something based on the authority of somebody else. It was what I felt inside of me that I was trying to deny for all those years, I think. The more you bring it out, the more, I think, it's a blossoming of your own personal spirituality. Your relationship with God comes out more as you develop as a person, as you mature. If you can do that.

The rules and regulations and all that that I grew up with in organized religion, I was getting all that mixed up with spirituality. Organized religion is important. I follow it. But I don't believe that it's necessary. I don't think that people who follow organized religion are necessarily spiritual. I think that there's a lot of people that are following organized religion that are not spiritual at all. So, I think it's okay if you want to follow it and be spiritual, but if you're following it just to follow it—which is what I was doing before—just following it to follow the rules, then I don't see how it can be spiritual. I don't see a connection. The spiritual is living a good life. So, I could go to church, and I could follow the rules, but if I'm going out the door, and I'm not practicing what I'm preaching, or I'm not feeling this relationship with God, well, then I'm not spiritual. It's in the relationship with God. I can talk about a relationship, but if I don't have it, then I'm not living it. Then I'm not spiritual.

One of my closest friends is a woman I met at the time of the crisis. She is someone who is spiritual. She is a divorced person, and as I thought then, not the kind of person that I would want to be friendly with. But she gave me God's message. I think I got God's message through her, and it was coming from a very unexpected avenue. She's a friend that made me really see God, really come to know Him. She does things charitably that I would never do. Like, I could follow the rules, but maybe I would be nasty to a person next to me. Like, say, not say hello, or judge them, or prejudge them. Now, she doesn't judge them, or she'll say hello. I just can't describe it. She's just a good person. She's very charitable, loving, kind, but also not a doormat. She doesn't let people walk all over her. She's empowered personally, so she's authentic, empowered personally and with a wonderful, trusting relationship with her God. And she gave that to me. Don't ask me how, but she did.

Maybe some people experience God through reading a very heavy book or something like that. I experience God through other people and through my feelings. I have intuitive feelings, or something, in connection with other people and myself and God. That's like what prayer is for me now. Prayer was . . . well, before it was rote, and earlier in life it was rote and also petition, asking for things but never really feeling like a center. And now prayer is more of a feeling and a center. I don't usually ask for anything. I usually ask that I'm open to God's will and that He shows me what He wants me to do. So, it's sort of like more of an openness and a pouring, like opening my hands and saying whatever. And it's more of a trusting. It's intuitive, and I don't know, but it feels more spiritual. It's not rote anymore at all. In fact, I can't even handle rote prayer anymore.

I don't have to go anywhere to find God. I think He's everywhere. I think He's in every relationship, and I think that He's all around me. You know, I don't think I have to go to a place to find God. Before, I would think to look for a church or possibly to kneel down to find Him. I have to center myself. I mean, if I'm out in the street, He's there, but I may not be aware of it. I have to calm down sometimes, and stop what I'm doing, and sort of like, just quiet myself. I mean, I could be out in the car, and He could be there. But if I'm in a hurried state or something, I'm not gonna feel His presence if I'm not stopping. Almost always in working with the problems of my students, I can feel His presence. I feel peaceful now, peaceful and calm.

Wendy

Wendy is a married woman with two grown daughters. Her life has had much more than its share of tragedy. Wendy's mother, with whom she had a wonderful relationship, died suddenly when Wendy was just six years old. After her mother died, her father was never the same, and he gradually became an alcoholic. He remarried, maybe for the sake of Wendy and her younger brother, but the stepmother was a "mean and selfish woman." All the time Wendy was growing up, there was a lot of chaos and neglect in the family. Also in AA, Wendy is a dynamic and generous woman at this point in her life. She has been sober for a number of years, and she is involved in the lives of her grandchildren and in her community. I asked her what her image of God was.

I don't . . . don't really know what it is. I know that it's very deep, and I have no idea. I have a sense of it. It's this universal thing that I just don't understand. I feel it's the spiritual world, and even that is a limited way of expressing it. My image in my mind always has been a visible light. Visible light is like a tiny bit on the spectrum of light. It's, like, the only way I can explain it. There's so much to it, but it just is, and somehow there's a part of me that has a sense of it, and I understand that it's there, and I feel that it's there, and I'm very comfortable with it. And I believe it is God. I use the word God because I don't know what else to use. It's, like, all encompassing. It's that whole thing.

To me it's really unconditional love—but even transcending that. It's just so much of what it is. It's so loving that it will be what people need and whatever their environment is, whatever their inner life is, whatever their religion is. It's a whole, and it is something that makes everything whole. Everything is incorporated in it. Someone, an individual person, me, whatever I need at the moment, God, this being, takes care of me. And He talks to me, and I talk to Him. You know, it's a Him. I was raised in a Christian tradition, so for me it is a Him. Sometimes, I need Him to be a long, white beard. Sometimes, He's my grandmother. Sometimes, He's . . . He's whatever image I feel comfortable with. It's sort of like He would be whatever. It's always a positive thing, and He always takes care of me. And that's just . . . I guess that's it.

I remember being very small. I can remember very far back—it's like I always knew this—sort of being in this great sea. Like the story in Hinduism or Buddhism where God is laying there sleeping, and He's sleeping in the lake, and it's warm, and it's comfortable, and I am there too. This warm, comfortable feeling. And it's like its always there and around me. And when I was little, I knew that it was always there around me, and it was all right, and I'd be taken care of. And then I had to learn about the material world, the world that I am in, and I use my senses to do that, my intellect, my brain. But there was this part of me that always was somehow in God. But I also had to go the other way, to learn how to cope in the world. And somehow part of that was my alcoholism. I had to learn the other side, which I don't think . . . I don't think is really a separate thing at all. I think it gives us compassion.

I have had this feeling really since I've been in the program that the things I did when I was drinking, the negative things, the things that I was ashamed of, were necessary for me to get to a place where I could get connected to God. I needed Him. And they were part of my learning about the world that I'm in. And once I recognized them, and I went through the shame of admitting them to people, then what it taught me was to connect to my real self. And it taught me compassion. It taught me so much. I don't think I would have really been able to feel part of the world, to feel that spiritual connection to the rest of the world, if I hadn't been through all this stuff.

I understand everything's two sides of the same thing. You know, it's like the dark side is just another side. It's a paradox. The bad is real, and we experience that, we have to experience that, but in a sense, the bad is not real at all. I had to immerse myself in the real world. It goes back to the visible light. Without pushing aside that sense of well-being, that knowing that God was there, that feeling that I was part of the greater whole, I could never . . . I could never fully know the light. This is hindsight stuff. This is how I see it now.

AA enabled me to return to my original self, but with this greater understanding. I really believe God picked me up and put me into this new life. It's like, "Okay, you've learned what you had to learn that way. Now I'll pick you up and put you here, and you'll do it this way." And it's really been like that for me. My journey is in the program. Before I came to the program, I was really in despair. It was sort of like I knew I had a problem with alcohol, but I had no idea what was happening. And I prayed and prayed for God to help me, even though I wasn't so sure then that there really was a God. And then one day, I woke up after I totaled my car—and did all these other terrible things—and I called AA. And I wound up in these rooms, and it got me back in touch with that feeling when I was younger. And I felt, once I was back in touch with it, that it had never really left.

There were a lot of other things that happened along the way. One thing was my grandmother. My grandmother had a great deal of faith, but she never really talked about it, never imposed it, if you know what I mean. But she had it, and it was always this very comforting thing that she had that I never really thought about when I was a kid. I mean she just had it, you know. And I remember one time when I was drinking, during my active years, I had this big, old blue car, and I was at my family's house, and I was pretty lit. I was supposed to drive her home, and I said, "Okay, I'll be coming out." It was a really cold night, and she was like seventy-five years old. So she goes out to the car, and she's waiting by the car.

Me, being the good alcoholic, I'm inside, taking forever to come out. And I come out a little more lit than I was when she went out, and I said, "I'm so sorry." And she looked at me, and she just said, "That's all right. I just said a prayer, and you came out." And I must have looked at her like, "What, are you nuts?" I must have had that look. Now, I loved her. I would never have attacked her that way. But I just spontaneously must have had that look. And she looked at me—a very wise lady—and she says, "I don't care if it's true or not. I believe in it." And that was a door for me. I remembered that a few years later when I came into the program. That was actually the beginning of me going back to my original state.

I want to be connected to all the aspects of God that are in different people. But my channels get blocked. I get caught in all the turmoil which usually has nothing to do with the present moment. It has to do with my emotions. But I find myself in AA. I get centered. I enter the present moment. Once I enter the present moment, then I'm okay. Once I get into the present moment, then I can see things in more of a perspective. And listening to other people tell their truth, whatever that may be, I mean even if they're sitting there telling me these horrible things that they did, I just sense that this is the truth, and that centers me. The truth will set you free. I have this habit that I developed when I go to meetings; my thing is to just listen, just listen and try to let it enter me. And within half an hour or forty-five minutes, it just comes in. I get lost in it, and there I am.

At a Speaker's Meeting someone said that the word "Yahweh" means "I am." I don't know how real this is, but it is very powerful to me. He's Himself, and He wants you to be yourself. He just wants to know. He doesn't want you, like, editing it or anything. He just wants to know. So, you have to know yourself. Unless you know your dark side and your truth, there's no need to follow God.

15

CONCLUSION

This book begins and ends with two basic questions. The first is, *why is our relating to God so often presented as if it were static and not something meant to develop as we ourselves develop and mature?* The second is, *why are so many adults still living with a God of childhood and adolescence, a Superego God?*

The methodological response to these two questions—the foundation of this book—lies in two crucial definitions: the definition of religion and the definition of adulthood. Religion is defined as "that which is about the self and God together." Religion is not about God, and it is not about the self. Religion is about "the self and God together." Adulthood is defined as "an integral self-in-mutuality." An adult self is not a separate, autonomous self, and an adult self is no longer at the mercy of the superego. An adult self is a whole self relating in mutuality to what is other.

The working response to these two questions—the structure of this book—lies in the description of two basic paradigms of "the self and God together." The first paradigm, "The Superego God," describes a subject-object understanding of the self in its togetherness with God. This is a distanced togetherness, an incomplete togetherness, and often an uneasy and conflicted togetherness—because the self is not yet its fullness, because God is not yet God's fullness, and because the process of imaging that relates this self to God is not yet its fullness. The second paradigm, "The Living God," is a harmonious understanding of the self in its togetherness with God. This is a close togetherness, a complete togetherness, and really an animating and mystical togetherness—because the self is now its fullness, because God is now God's fullness, and because the process of imaging that relates this self to God is now its fullness.

The final response to these two questions—the dynamic in this book—lies in the experience of transformation. Our imaging of God is meant to be transformed as we grow and develop. An adolescing self is meant to be transformed into an adult self. Fettered imaging is meant to be transformed into unfettered imaging. The Superego God is meant to be transformed into the Living God. If we begin, as we usually do, with the paradigm of the Superego God, we are not meant to end there. The paradigm of "The Superego God" is an incomplete paradigm. It is meant to be transformed into the paradigm of "The Living God."

Finally, some conclusions can be drawn from asking these two questions—conclusions that are primarily pastoral and practical.

1. *An adult self is essential for adult religion.* Perhaps the single most important finding of these pages is that the structure of adult religion depends on the structure of adulthood. Human development is not optional if we want to be fully religious. Without an adult self as an integral self-in-mutuality, there is no adult religion. On the one hand, this finding can be easily understood. If a person is not an adult, why would we suppose that he or she would have an adult relationship with God? On the other hand, of all the factors that seem to be important in the life of religion as it is usually thought about, adult development is rarely taken into account.

2. *Human development and religious development cannot be separated.* This finding, even though it is a working supposition of these pages, is confirmed most clearly in the way that we develop as a process of imaging. The fettered imaging of the adolescing self—with its fantasy, relating in transference, and logic of objective knowing—is operative in our grasp of religious reality, just as it is in our grasp of any other aspect of reality. Fettered imaging is going to find a Superego God. Likewise, the unfettered imaging of the adult self—an adult, integral process of imaging—is operative in our grasp of religious reality, just as it is in our grasp of any other aspect of reality. With unfettered imaging,

we are capable of finding a Living God. As a process of imaging, human development and religious development are meant to go hand in hand.

3. Adult religious experiencing is mystical experiencing. Of all the findings of these pages, the understanding that adult religion is mystical experiencing is perhaps the most interesting and the most challenging. Adult religion is about the unity of "the self and God together." To know the self is to know God, and to know God is to know the self. The language of "subject-object," the language of "otherness," the language of "two" does not work very well in adult religion. In adult religion, the experiencing of God is in terms of a mutuality and an intimacy in which two gives way to one. This is a paradox that can be spoken of only in metaphor.

4. Religion is that which is about the self and God together. Again, even though this definition of religion is a starting point for this book, it is also a conclusion. In adult religion, this conclusion can be seen clearly because in adult religion the self and God are together in a way in which separation cannot get a foothold. Freud started with the subject-object dichotomy, with an understanding of adolescing religion in terms of fantasy, relating in transference, and the logic of objective knowing. Because of this dichotomy, he was never able to find an adult religion in which the self and God necessarily go together. To understand religion, we need to experience the depth and the mystery of the Living God. Adolescing religion, by its very nature, is only the first part of the journey toward that understanding.

5. Adult religion is possible when adolescing religion is transformed. This is perhaps the most practical finding of these pages. Adult religion, at least for many of us, is realized only though considerable personal struggle. The Superego God does not magically turn into the Living God as we grow up. For many of us, it seems, fantasy, relating in transference, and the logic of objective knowing are amazingly powerful obstacles in the way of adult religion, obstacles that often can be overcome only by sustained attention, conscious effort, and the help, example, and empathy of those who are at home with a Living God.

6. Adult religion is an integral spirituality. One of the most clarifying findings of these pages is that the structure of adulthood is the structure of a whole or integral spirituality. While religion and spirituality are related in that they are both able to give meaning to life, adult religion is not an integral spirituality because it is religious. Adult religion is an integral spirituality because it is adult. If an integral spirituality provides an adult self with meaning for life and relates it to a larger whole, then in adult religion, we find the meaning and the larger whole in God.

7. *Mutuality, experience, and mystery are essential for adult religion.* True mutuality, a genuine respect for each person's experience of God, and an openness to mystery are hallmarks of adult religion on the personal level and on the organizational level as well. While authoritarianism, rationalism, and anthropomorphism can be extremely powerful in organized religion, when we are adult selves with an unfettered imaging of God, we are able to stand as an even more powerful challenge to these fettered structures. Adult selves with an unfettered imaging of God are a living testament to the reality of mutuality, experience, and mystery in organized religion. When we are adult selves with an integral imaging of God, we are able to embody in ourselves and for each other a spirituality of the Living God.

What John Glaser says in the quote that begins this book is true:

> To associate the mystery of invitation, the absolute yes to man's [*sic*] future, the radical call to eternally abiding love—God—with the hot and cold arbitrary tyrant of the superego is a matter of grave distortion.

Our imaging of God must be adequate for the reality of who God is. Our imaging of God must be adequate for the reality of who we are. On both counts, the paradigm of "The Superego God" falls short. Only the paradigm of "The Living God" can do justice to our ability to become the selves we are meant to be. Only the paradigm of "The Living God" can do justice to our ability to image the reality of God. Only the paradigm of "The Living God" is a spirituality for adults.

BIBLIOGRAPHY

Angyal, Andras. "The Convergence of Psychotherapy and Religion." *The Journal of Pastoral Care* 5, no. 4 (1951): 4–14.

Augustinus, Aurelius. *Confessiones.*

———. *Soliloquies.*

Barrett, Deborah A. "Suffering and the Process of Transformation." *The Journal of Pastoral Care* 53, no. 4 (Winter 1999): 461–72.

Basseches, Michael. *Dialectical Thinking and Adult Development.* Norwood, NJ: Ablex, 1984.

Becker, Ernest. *The Denial of Death.* New York: Free Press, 1973.

Becker, William H. "Spiritual Struggle in Contemporary America." *Theology Today* 51 (July 1994): 256–69.

Bianchi, Eugene C., and Rosemary R. Ruether. *From Machismo to Mutuality: Essays on Sexism and Man-Woman Liberation.* New York: Paulist Press, 1976.

Bilotta, Vincent M., III. "Originality, Ordinary Intimacy and the Spiritual Life: Welcome! Make Yourself At-home." *Studies in Formative Spirituality* 1, no. 1 (February 1980): 83–91.

Blasi, Augusto. "Identity and the Development of the Self." In *Self, Ego, and Identity: Integrative Approaches*, edited by Daniel K. Lapsley and F. Clark Power, 220–42. New York: Springer-Verlag, 1988.

Booth, Leo. *When God Becomes a Drug: Breaking the Chains of Religious Addiction and Abuse.* Los Angeles: Tarcher, 1991.

Bragan, Kenneth. *Self and Spirit in the Therapeutic Relationship.* London: Routledge, 1996.

Bryant, Christopher. *Depth Psychology and Religious Belief.* London: Darton, Longman & Todd, 1987.

———. *Jung and the Christian Way.* Minneapolis, MN: Seabury Press, 1984.

Buber, Martin. *The Knowledge of Man,* translated by Maurice Friedman and Ronald Gregor Smith. New York: Harper & Row, 1965.

Campbell, Peter A., and Edwin M. McMahon. *Bio-Spirituality: Focusing as a Way to Grow.* 2nd ed. Chicago: Loyola Press, 1997.

Canda, Edward R. "Spirituality, Religious Diversity, and Social Work Practice." *Social Casework* 69, no. 4 (1988): 238–47.

Casey, Edward S. *Spirit and Soul: Essays in Philosophical Psychology.* Dallas, TX: Spring, 1991.

Caspary, William R. "The Concept of a Core-Self." In *The Book of the Self: Person, Pretext, and Process,* edited by Polly Young-Eisendrath and James A. Hall, 366–81. New York: New York University Press, 1987.

Cavell, Marcia. "Erik Erikson and the Temporal Mind." In *Ideas and Identities: The Life and Work of Erik Erikson,* edited by Robert S. Wallerstein and Leo Goldberger, 33–47. Madison, CT: International Universities Press, 1998.

Clifford, Paul R. "The Place of Feeling in Religious Awareness." In *New Theology, No. 7: The Recovery of Transcendence,* edited by Martin E. Marty and Dean G. Peerman, 47–55. New York: Macmillan, 1970.

Conn, Joann W. *Spirituality and Personal Maturity.* New York: Paulist Press, 1989.

Crossan, John Dominic. "Paradox Gives Rise to Metaphor: Paul Ricoeur's Hermeneutics and the Parables of Jesus." *Biblical Research* 24/25 (1979–1980): 20–37.

———. "Stages in Imagination." In *The Archaeology of the Imagination.* Thematic Series, edited by Charles E. Winquist. *Journal of the American Academy of Religion* 48, no. 2 (1981): 49–62.

Csordas, Thomas J. "Embodiment as a Paradigm for Anthropology." *Ethos* 18, no. 1 (1990): 5–47.

Desmond, William. *Perplexity and Ultimacy: Metaphysical Thoughts from the Middle.* New York: State University of New York Press, 1995.

Elhard, Leland. "Living Faith: Some Contributions of the Concept of Ego-identity to the Understanding of Faith." In *The Dialogue between Theology and Psychology,* edited by Peter Homans, 135–61. Chicago: University of Chicago Press, 1968.

Erikson, Erik H. *Childhood and Society.* 2nd ed. New York: Norton, 1963.

———. *Identity: Youth and Crisis.* New York: Norton, 1968.

——. *Identity and the Life Cycle*. New York: Norton, 1980.

——. *Insight and Responsibility*. New York: Norton, 1964.

——. *Toys and Reasons: Stages in the Ritualization of Experience*. New York: Norton, 1977.

Ewing, James W. "The Pastoral Therapeutic Stance." In *Psychiatry, Ministry and Pastoral Counseling*, edited by A. W. Richard Sipe and Clarence J. Rowe, 64–77. Collegeville, MN: The Liturgical Press, 1984.

Faiver, Christopher, R. Elliott Ingersoll, Eugene M. O'Brien, and Christopher McNally. *Explorations in Counseling and Spirituality: Philosophical, Practical, and Personal Reflections*. Belmont, CA: Brooks/Cole, 2001.

Fischer, Kathleen R. *Reclaiming the Connection: A Contemporary Spirituality*. Kansas City, MO: Sheed & Ward, 1990.

Fowler, James W. *Stages of Faith: The Psychology of Human Development and the Quest for Meaning*. San Francisco: Harper & Row, 1981.

Frankl, Viktor E. *The Doctor and the Soul*. New York: Knopf, 1966.

——. *Psychotherapy and Existentialism*. New York: Washington Square Press, 1967.

——. *The Will to Meaning: Foundations and Applications of Logotherapy*. New York: New American Library, 1969.

Freud, Sigmund. *The Future of an Illusion*. Garden City, NY: Anchor, 1964.

——. *New Introductory Lectures on Psychoanalysis*, translated and edited by James Strachey. New York: Norton, 1965.

Gallagher, Kenneth T. *The Philosophy of Gabriel Marcel*. New York: Fordham University Press, 1962.

Geertz, Clifford. "On the Nature of Anthropological Understanding." *American Scientist* 63 (1975): 47–53.

Gendlin, Eugene T. "Experiencing: A Variable in the Process of Therapeutic Change." *The American Journal of Psychotherapy* 15, no. 2 (April 1961): 233–45.

——. *Focusing*. New York: Bantam, 1981.

——. *Focusing-Oriented Psychotherapy: A Manual of the Experiential Method*. New York: Guilford, 1996.

——. "A Theory of Personality Change." In *New Directions in Client-Centered Therapy*, edited by J. T. Hart and T. M. Tomlinson, 129–73. Boston: Houghton Mifflin, 1970.

Gill, Jerry H. *Mediated Transcendence: A Postmodern Reflection*. Macon, GA: Mercer University Press, 1989.

——. *Merleau-Ponty and Metaphor*. Atlantic Highlands, NJ: Humanities Press, 1991.

———. *On Knowing God*. Philadelphia: Westminster Press, 1981.

Glaser, John W. "Conscience and Superego: A Key Distinction." In *Conscience: Theological and Psychological Perspectives*, edited by C. Ellis Nelson, 167–88. New York: Newman, 1973.

Grant, Robert. *The Way of the Wound: A Spirituality of Trauma and Transformation*. Oakland, CA: Robert Grant, 1996.

Grey, Mary. "Falling into Freedom: Searching for a New Interpretation of Sin in a Secular Society." *Scottish Journal of Theology* 47, no. 2 (1994): 223–43.

Grimes, Ronald L. *Deeply into the Bone: Re-inventing Rites of Passage*. Berkeley: University of California Press, 2002.

Hardiman, Michael. *Ordinary Heroes: A Future for Men*. Dublin: Newleaf, 2000.

Harvey, Nicholas P. "Christian Morality and Pastoral Theology." In *The Blackwell Reader in Pastoral and Practical Theology*, edited by James Woodward and Stephen Pattison, 182–91. Malden, MA: Blackwell, 2000.

Hekman, Susan. *Moral Voices, Moral Selves: Carol Gilligan and Feminist Moral Theory*. University Park: Pennsylvania State University Press, 1995.

Herman, Judith L. *Trauma and Recovery*. New York: Basic Books, 1992.

Heron, John. *Feeling and Personhood: Psychology in Another Key*. London: Sage, 1992.

Hillman, James. *The Thought of the Heart*. Dallas, TX: Spring, 1984.

Himes, Michael J. *Doing the Truth in Love: Conversations about God, Relationships and Service*. New York: Paulist, 1995.

Hinterkopf, Elfie. *Integrating Spirituality in Counseling: A Manual for Using the Experiential Focusing Method*. Alexandria, VA: American Counseling Association, 1998.

Holmes, Urban T. *Spirituality for Ministry*. New York: Harper & Row, 1982.

Homans, Peter. "Toward a Psychology of Religion: By Way of Freud and Tillich." In *The Dialogue between Theology and Psychology*, edited by Peter Homans, 53–81. Chicago: University of Chicago Press, 1968.

———. "Transference and Transcendence: Freud and Tillich on the Nature of Personal Relatedness." *Journal of Religion* 46, no. 1, pt. 2 (1966): 148–64.

Huff, Margaret C. "The Interdependent Self: An Integrated Concept from Feminist Theology and Feminist Psychology." *Philosophy & Theology* 11, no. 2 (Winter 1987): 160–72.

Hulme, William E. *Pastoral Care and Counseling: Using the Unique Resources of the Christian Tradition.* Minneapolis, MN: Augsburg, 1981.

Jacobi, Mario. *The Analytic Encounter: Transference and Human Relationship.* Toronto: Inner City Books, 1984.

James, William. *The Varieties of Religious Experience.* Cambridge, MA: Harvard University Press, 1985.

Jernigan, Homer L. "Spirituality in Older Adults: A Cross-Cultural and Interfaith Perspective." *Pastoral Psychology* 49 (2001): 413–37.

Johnson, Elizabeth A. *She Who Is: The Mystery of God in Feminist Discourse.* New York: Crossroad, 1992.

Johnson, Mark. *The Body in the Mind: The Bodily Basis of Meaning, Imagination, and Reason.* Chicago: University of Chicago Press, 1987.

Jordan, Judith V. "Empathy and Self Boundaries." In *Women's Growth in Connection: Writings from the Stone Center,* edited by Judith V. Jordan, Alexandra G. Kaplan, Jean Baker Miller, Irene P. Stiver, and Janet L. Surrey, 67–80. New York: Guilford, 1991.

———. "The Meaning of Mutuality." In *Women's Growth in Connection: Writings from the Stone Center,* edited by Judith V. Jordan, Alexandra G. Kaplan, Jean Baker Miller, Irene P. Stiver, and Janet L. Surrey, 81–96. New York: Guilford, 1991.

Jordan, Judith V., Alexandra G. Kaplan, Jean Baker Miller, Irene P. Stiver, and Janet L. Surrey, eds. *Women's Growth in Connection: Writings from the Stone Center.* New York: Guilford, 1991.

Joyce, Vivienne. "The Play of Illusion as an Opening to the Future of the Self: Reflections of a Religious Clinician Occasioned by Rereading *The Future of an Illusion.*" In *Psychotherapy and the Religiously Committed Patient,* edited by E. Mark Stern, 71–77. New York: Haworth, 1985.

Jung, Carl G. *The Collected Works of C. G. Jung.* Vol. 9, pt. 2, *Aion: Researches into the Phenomenology of the Self.* Princeton, NJ: Princeton University Press, 1979.

———. *The Collected Works of C. G. Jung.* Vol. 9, pt. 1, *Archetypes and the Collective Unconscious.* Princeton, NJ: Princeton University Press, 1968.

———. "The Development of Personality." Chap. 7 in *The Collected Works of C. G. Jung.* Vol. 17, *The Development of Personality.* Princeton, NJ: Princeton University Press, 1981.

———. *Psychology and Religion.* New Haven, CT: Yale University Press, 1938.

Kalsched, Donald. *The Inner World of Trauma: Archetypal Defenses of the Personal Spirit.* New York: Routledge, 1996.

Kao, Charles C. L. "Maturity, Spirituality, and Theological Reconstruction." In *Maturity and the Quest for Spiritual Meaning*, edited by Charles C. L. Kao, 41–52. Lanham, MD: University Press of America, 1988.

Kaufman, Gordon D. "Mystery, Critical Consciousness, and Faith." In *The Rationality of Religious Belief*, edited by William J. Abraham and Steven W. Holtzer, 53–69. Oxford: Clarendon, 1987.

Kearney, Richard. *The Wake of the Imagination: Toward a Postmodern Culture*. Minneapolis: University of Minnesota Press, 1988.

Keating, Thomas. *Intimacy with God*. New York: Crossroad, 1994.

Kegan, Robert. *The Evolving Self: Problem and Process in Human Development*. Cambridge, MA: Harvard University Press, 1982.

Kelly, Eugene W., Jr. *Spirituality and Religion in Counseling and Psychotherapy: Diversity in Theory and Practice*. Alexandria, VA: American Counseling Association, 1995.

King, J. Norman. *Experiencing God All Ways and Every Day*. Minneapolis, MN: Winston, 1982.

Kirschner, Suzanne R. *The Religious and Romantic Origins of Psychoanalysis: Individuation and Integration in Post-Freudian Theory*. New York: Cambridge University Press, 1996.

Knowles, Richard T. *Human Development and Human Possibility: Erikson in the Light of Heidegger*. Lanham, MD: University Press of America, 1986.

Kohlberg, Lawrence. *The Philosophy of Moral Development: Moral Stages and the Idea of Development*. San Francisco: Harper & Row, 1981.

Kopas, Jane. *Sacred Identity: Exploring a Theology of the Person*. New York: Paulist, 1994.

Koplowitz, Herb. "Unitary Thought: A Projection beyond Piaget's Formal Operations Stage." Manuscript, Addiction Research Foundation, Simcoe, Ontario, May 1978.

Kornfeld, Margaret. *Cultivating Wholeness: A Guide to Care and Counseling in Faith Communities*. New York: Continuum, 1998.

Kornfield, Jack. *A Path with Heart: A Guide through the Perils and Promises of Spiritual Life*. New York: Bantam, 1993.

Krieger, Jonathan. "The Concept of the Object Scale and Cognitive Style: Measures of Differentiation and Their Relationship to Empathy." PhD diss., Fordham University, 1988.

Kunz, George. *The Paradox of Power and Weakness: Levinas and an Alternative Paradigm for Psychology*. Albany: State University of New York Press, 1998.

Lakoff, George, and Mark Johnson. *Philosophy in the Flesh: The Embodied Mind and Its Challenge to Western Thought.* New York: Basic Books, 1999.

Lash, Nicholas. "Incarnate and Determinate Freedom." In *On Freedom,* edited by Leroy S. Rouner, 15–29. Notre Dame, IN: University of Notre Dame Press, 1989.

Leder, Drew. *The Absent Body.* Chicago: University of Chicago Press, 1990.

Leean, Constance. "Spiritual and Psychological Life Cycle Tapestry." *Religious Education* 83, no. 1 (Winter 1988): 45–51.

LeShan, Lawrence. *How to Meditate: A Guide to Self-Discovery.* New York: Bantam, 1974.

Levin, David M. "Eros and Psyche: A Reading of Neumann and Merleau-Ponty." In *Pathways into the Jungian World: Phenomenology and Analytical Psychology,* edited by Roger Brooke, 161–78. New York: Routledge, 2000.

Levin, Jeff. "'Bumping the Top': Is Mysticism the Future of Religious Gerontology?" In *Aging, Spirituality, and Religion: A Handbook,* edited by Melvin A. Kimble and Susan H. McFadden, Vol. 2, 402–11. Minneapolis, MN: Fortress, 2003.

Loevinger, Jane, with the assistance of Augusto Blasi. *Ego Development: Conceptions and Theories.* San Francisco: Jossey-Bass, 1976.

Macmurray, John. *Persons in Relation.* London: Faber and Faber, 1961.

McDargh, John. "God, Mother and Me: An Object Relational Perspective on Religious Material." *Pastoral Psychology* 34, no. 4 (Summer 1986): 251–63.

Marcel, Gabriel. *Homo Viator: Introduction to a Metaphysic of Hope.* New York: Harper & Row, 1962.

———. *Metaphysical Journal.* Chicago: Regnery, 1952.

———. *The Mystery of Being.* 2 vols. Chicago: Regnery, 1960.

Marcia, James E. "Common Processes Underlying Ego Identity, Cognitive/Moral Development, and Individuation." In *Self, Ego, and Identity: Integrative Approaches,* edited by Daniel K. Lapsley and F. Clark Power, 211–25. New York: Springer-Verlag, 1988.

Maslow, Abraham H. *Religions, Values, Peak Experiences.* New York: Viking Compass, 1970.

———. "A Theory of Human Motivation." In *Motivation and Personality,* 35–58. 2nd ed. New York: Harper & Row, 1976.

May, Gerald G. *Will and Spirit: A Contemplative Psychology.* San Francisco: Harper & Row, 1982.

Meissner, W. W. *Psychoanalysis and Religious Experience.* New Haven, CT: Yale University Press, 1984.

Merton, Thomas. *Spiritual Direction and Meditation.* Collegeville, MN: The Liturgical Press, 1960.

——. "To Ripu Daman Lama." In *The Hidden Ground of Love: The Letters of Thomas Merton on Religious Experience and Social Concerns,* selected and edited by William H. Shannon, 451–53. New York: Farrar, Straus and Giroux, 1985.

Moore, Robert, and Douglas Gillette. *King, Warrior, Magician, Lover: Rediscovering the Archetypes of the Mature Masculine.* San Francisco: HarperSanFrancisco, 1990.

Moore, Thomas. *Care of the Soul: A Guide for Cultivating Depth and Sacredness in Everyday Life.* New York: HarperCollins, 1992.

Myers, Barbara K. *Young Children and Spirituality.* London: Routledge, 1997.

Nakken, Craig. *The Addictive Personality: Understanding Compulsion in Our Lives.* New York: HarperCollins, 1988.

Nelson, James. *Between Two Gardens: Reflections on Sexuality and Religious Experience.* New York: Pilgrim, 1983.

Nelson, Katherine, Darah Hensler, and Daniela Plesa. "Entering a Community of Minds." In *Toward a Feminist Developmental Psychology,* edited by Patricia H. Miller and Ellen K. Scholnick, 61–83. New York: Routledge, 2000.

Nelson, Susan L. "Soul-Loss and Sin: A Dance of Alienation." In *On Losing the Soul: Essays in the Social Psychology of Religion,* edited by Richard K. Fenn and Donald Capps, 97–116. Albany: State University of New York Press, 1995.

Niebuhr, H. Richard. "The Responsibility of the Church for Society." In *The Gospel, the Church, and the World,* edited by Kenneth Scott Latourette, 111–33. New York: Harper & Brothers, 1946.

Noam, Gil G. "Beyond Freud and Piaget: Biographical Worlds—Interpersonal Self." In *The Moral Domain,* edited by Thomas E. Wren, 361–99. Cambridge, MA: MIT Press, 1990.

Nothwehr, Dawn M. *Mutuality: A Formal Norm for Christian Ethics.* San Francisco: Catholic Scholars Press, 1998.

Oliver, Harold H. *Relatedness: Essays in Metaphysics and Theology.* Macon, GA: Mercer University Press, 1984.

Ots, Thomas. "The Silenced Body—The Expressive *Leib*: On the Dialectic of Mind and Life in Chinese Cathartic Healing." In *Embodiment and Ex-*

perience: The Existential Ground of Culture and Self, edited by Thomas J. Csordas, 116–36. New York: Cambridge University Press, 1994.

Palmer, Parker. *The Active Life: A Spirituality of Work, Creativity, and Caring*. San Francisco: Jossey-Bass, 1990.

———. *Let Your Life Speak: Listening for the Voice of Vocation*. San Francisco: Jossey-Bass, 2000.

Parks, Sharon Daloz. *Big Questions, Worthy Dreams*. San Francisco: Jossey-Bass, 2000.

Peck, Scott. *Further along the Road Less Traveled: The Unending Journey toward Spiritual Growth*. New York: Simon & Schuster, 1993.

Philibert, Paul J. "Readiness for Ritual: Psychological Aspects of Maturity in Christian Celebration." In *Alternative Futures for Worship*, edited by Regis A. Duffy, 63–121. Collegeville, MN: The Liturgical Press, 1987.

Piaget, Jean. *Genetic Epistemology*. New York: Norton, 1971.

———. *Six Psychological Studies*, translated by Anita Tenzer. New York: Vintage, 1968.

Progoff, Ira. *At a Journal Workshop*. Los Angeles: Tarcher, 1992.

———. *Depth Psychology and Modern Man*. New York: McGraw-Hill, 1973.

———. *The Symbolic and the Real*. New York: McGraw-Hill, 1963.

Pruyser, Paul W. *Between Belief and Unbelief*. New York: Harper & Row, 1974.

———. "Lessons from Art Theory for the Psychology of Religion." *Journal for the Scientific Study of Religion* 15, no. 1 (March 1976): 1–14.

———. "Psychological Roots and Branches of Belief." *Pastoral Psychology* 28, no. 1 (Fall 1979): 8–20.

———. "Sigmund Freud and His Legacy: Psychoanalytic Psychology of Religion." In *Beyond the Classics? Essays in the Scientific Study of Religion*, edited by Charles Y. Glock and Phillip E. Hammond, 243–90. New York: Harper & Row, 1973.

———. "The Tutored Imagination in Religion." In *Changing Views of the Human Condition*, edited by Paul W. Pruyser, 101–15. Macon, GA: Mercer University Press, 1987.

Rhodes, Lynn. *Co-Creating: A Feminist Vision of Ministry*. Philadelphia: Westminster, 1987.

Ricoeur, Paul. *Oneself as Another*. Chicago: University of Chicago Press, 1992.

Rizzuto, Ana-Maria. *The Birth of the Living God*. Chicago: University of Chicago Press, 1979.

Rogers, Carl R. "Paul Tillich and Carl Rogers: A Dialogue." *Pastoral Psychology* 19 (February 1968): 55–64.

————. "A Process Conception of Psychotherapy." Chap. 7 in *On Becoming a Person*. Boston: Houghton Mifflin, 1961.

————. "A Theory of Therapy, Personality, and Interpersonal Relationships, as Developed in the Client-Centered Framework." In *Psychology: A Study of a Science*, edited by Sigmund Koch, Vol. 3, *Formulations of the Person and the Social Context*, 184–256. New York: McGraw-Hill, 1959.

————. "The Therapist's View of the Good Life: The Fully Functioning Person." Chap. 9 in *On Becoming a Person*, 184–96. Boston: Houghton Mifflin, 1961.

Romanyshyn, Robert D. "Alchemy and the Subtle Body of Metaphor." In *Pathways into the Jungian World: Phenomenology and Analytical Psychology*, edited by Roger Brooke, 27–47. New York: Routledge, 2000.

Ross, Maggie. *Pillars of Flame: Power, Priesthood, and Spiritual Maturity*. San Francisco: Harper & Row, 1988.

Rümke, H. C. *The Psychology of Unbelief*, translated by M. H. C. Willems. New York: Sheed and Ward, 1962.

Schachtel, Ernest G. *Metamorphosis: On the Development of Affect, Perception, Attention, and Memory*. New York: Basic Books, 1959.

Schecter, David E. "The Loving and Persecuting Superego." *Contemporary Psychoanalysis* 15, no. 3 (1979): 361–79.

Scheler, Max. *Man's Place in Nature*. New York: Noonday, 1962.

Schneiders, Sandra M. "The Contemporary Ministry of Spiritual Direction." *Chicago Studies* 15 (Spring 1976): 119–35.

Selman, Robert. *The Growth of Interpersonal Understanding: Developmental and Clinical Analyses*. New York: Academic Press, 1980.

Shea, John J. "Adult Faith, Pastoral Counseling, and Spiritual Direction." *The Journal of Pastoral Care* 51, no. 3 (Fall 1997): 259–70.

————. "The Adult Self: Process and Paradox." *Journal of Adult Development* 10, no. 1 (January 2003): 23–30.

————. "Adulthood—A Missing Perspective: Psychotherapy, Spirituality, and Religion." *American Journal of Pastoral Counseling* 7, no. 1 (2004): 39–65.

————. "The Impact of Chemical Addiction on the Realization of an Adult Self." Unpublished study, Fordham University, 1997.

————. *Religious Experiencing: William James and Eugene Gendlin*. Lanham, MD: University Press of America, 1987.

Silesius, Angelus. *The Cherubinic Wanderer*, translated by Maria Shrady. New York: Paulist Press, 1986.

Singer, June. *Seeing through the Visible World*. San Francisco: Harper & Row, 1990.

Sloan, Tod. *Life Choices: Understanding Dilemmas and Decisions*. Boulder, CO: Westview, 1996.

Soskice, Janet. "Knowledge and Experience in Science and Religion: Can We Be Realists?" In *Physics, Philosophy, and Theology: Common Quest for Understanding*, edited by Robert J. Russell, William R. Stoeger, and George V. Coyne, 173–84. Notre Dame, IN: University of Notre Dame Press and Vatican Observatory, 1988.

Souvaine, Emily, Lisa L. Lahey, and Robert Kegan. "Life after Formal Operations: Implications for a Psychology of the Self." In *Higher Stages of Human Development: Perspectives on Adult Growth*, edited by Charles N. Alexander and Ellen J. Langer, 229–57. New York: Oxford, 1990.

Spero, Moshe H. *Religious Objects as Psychological Structures: A Critical Integration of Object Relations Theory, Psychotherapy, and Judaism*. Chicago: University of Chicago Press, 1992.

Stein, Murray. *Transformation: Emergence of the Self*. College Station: Texas A&M University, 1998.

Stephen, Karin. "Relations between the Superego and the Ego." *Psychoanalysis and History* 21, no. 1 (2000): 11–28.

Stewart, Abigail J., and Joseph M. Healy, Jr. "Processing Affective Responses to Life Experiences: The Development of the Adult Self." In *Emotion in Adult Development*, edited by Carol Z. Malatesta and Carroll E. Izard, 277–95. London: Sage, 1984.

Suzuki, D. T. *Zen Buddhism*. New York: Doubleday, 1956.

Taylor, Charles. *Sources of the Self: The Making of the Modern Identity*. Cambridge, MA: Harvard University Press, 1989.

Taylor, Mark C. *Journeys to Selfhood: Hegel & Kierkegaard*. New York: Fordham University Press, 2000.

Thérèse of Lisieux. *Autobiography of a Saint*, translated by Ronald Knox. London: Harvill, 1958.

Ticho, Ernst A. "The Development of Superego Autonomy." *The Psychoanalytic Review* 59, no. 2 (Summer 1972): 217–33.

Tickerhoof, Bernard. *Paradox: The Spiritual Path to Transformation*. Mystic, CT: Twenty-third Publications, 2002.

Tilley, Christopher. *Metaphor and Material Culture*. Oxford: Blackwell, 1999.

Tillich, Paul. *The Courage to Be*. New Haven, CT: Yale University Press, 1952.

Ulanov, Ann B. *The Wisdom of the Psyche*. Cambridge, MA: Cowley, 1988.

Ulanov, Ann, and Barry Ulanov. *Religion and the Unconscious*. Philadelphia: Westminster, 1975.

Van Dusen, Wilson. *The Natural Depth in Man*. New York: Harper & Row, 1972.

van Manen, Max, and Bas Levering. *Childhood's Secrets: Intimacy, Privacy, and the Self Reconsidered*. New York: Teachers College Press, 1996.

Vergote, Antoine. "Confrontation with Neutrality in Theory and Practice." In *Psychoanalysis and Religion*, edited by Joseph H. Smith and Susan A. Handelman, 74–94. Baltimore: Johns Hopkins University Press, 1990.

Watts, Fraser, and Mark Williams. *The Psychology of Religious Knowing*. London: Geoffrey Chapman, 1994.

Westley, Dick. *Redemptive Intimacy: A New Perspective for the Journey to Adult Faith*. Mystic, CT: Twenty-third Publications, 1981.

Wilder, Amos Niven. *Theopoetic: Theology and the Religious Imagination*. Philadelphia: Fortress, 1976.

Willeford, William. *Feeling, Imagination, and the Self: Transformations of the Mother-Infant Relationship*. Evanston, IL: Northwestern University Press, 1987.

Wilshire, Bruce. *Role Playing and Identity: The Limits of Theatre as Metaphor*. Bloomington: Indiana University Press, 1982.

Winnicott, D. W. *Playing and Reality*. London: Routledge, 1982.

Wittgenstein, Ludwig. *Philosophical Investigations*, translated by G. E. M. Anscombe. Oxford: Blackwell, 1968.

Woodman, Marion. "In Her Own Voice: An Interview with Marion Woodman by Anne A. Simpkinson." *Common Boundary* 10, no. 4 (July/August 1992): 22–30.

Wuthnow, Robert. *Creative Spirituality: The Way of the Artist*. Berkeley: University of California Press, 2001.

INDEX

ABOUT THE AUTHOR

John J. Shea is a visiting associate professor of pastoral care and counseling at the Institute of Religious Education and Pastoral Ministry, Boston College.